Sissel Hansen
/ Startup Guide

Switzerland is known for its high quality of life and international culture, and the Basel Area is a key part of this reputation. One of the world's leading locations for life sciences, the region is home to pioneers in biotechnology, pharmaceuticals and digital health. Corporations, startups, universities and other organizations cooperate and support each other to create a strong and lively ecosystem that features a high level of education and specialized skills.

The cantons of Basel-Landschaft, Basel-Stadt and Jura each have their own unique qualities, but are united in creating a future-focused ecosystem. Basel Area Business & Innovation is a key player in the development of this community, providing numerous support programs and events to help both local and international entrepreneurs succeed here. The BaseLaunch incubator, which partners with scientists and entrepreneurs to help launch and grow biotech companies, is just one example of its initiatives.

There's also a wide range of coworking spaces that cater to every need in the Basel Area, from specialized facilities such as Technologiepark Basel to the relaxed and welcoming atmosphere of The Manhattan, located in charming Delémont.

An established epicenter of research, and with easy access to French and German markets, the Basel Area is an exciting place for entrepreneurs in healthcare and beyond to start or grow their venture. We're excited to share the stories of some of the region's startups, founders, investors, schools and programs, and hope that they inspire you.

Local Community Partner / Basel Area Business & Innovation

Basel Area – isn't that the region with lots of life sciences companies nestled along the River Rhine, right at the border of France and Germany?

Yes, you are right. We are proud of our life sciences industry, which has been shaping our region for centuries and has evolved into a booming healthcare industry. It is the foundation of what we see today: a thriving business and startup hub.

Thanks to the life sciences industry, excellent universities and research institutions, the Basel Area has evolved into a magnet for talent. That talent is exploring its options in the startup world. Basel Area Business & Innovation and the cantons of Basel-Landschaft, Basel-Stadt and Jura make sure that founders and entrepreneurs get all the support they need to succeed in their endeavors here. And yes, our services are free of charge.

To give you an idea of what we can do for an aspiring founder: you want to know how to set up a company in Switzerland – we guide you through the steps. A startup is looking for investors – we make sure to set founders up with coaches, get them ready to pitch and connect them to investors. Entrepreneurs want to find talent, peers or partners – we introduce them to the local startup ecosystem. A company from abroad needs an office – we know the facilities and offerings. With state-of-the-art coworking spaces and technology and innovation parks, we offer a variety of spaces and laboratories that will place you in the middle of our community.

Whether you are a local player or putting your toes into foreign waters, this community in the Basel Area is a force of nature, taking you with it like the River Rhine. We invite you to take a swim.

Christof Klöpper
CEO
Basel Area Business & Innovation

Local Community Partner / Basel Area Business & Innovation

Basel Area Business & Innovation is a nonprofit agency dedicated to helping startups, institutions and companies find business success in the Basel Area. As an independent organization funded by the cantons of Basel-Landschaft, Basel-Stadt and Jura, as well as by the Swiss government and private foundations, it helps develop a robust business climate and supports innovative ventures.

The Basel Area is a fast-growing ecosystem for startups and entrepreneurs. It is often ranked high in international rankings due to its high level of talent, quality of life, market access, administrative efficiency and supportive government, which combine to provide high stability.

Global leaders, including Novartis, Roche, Fossil, Bayer, Ricola, Dufry and Panalpina, among others, are based in the Basel region. But it's not only big corporations that are here to innovate and grow. The Basel Area has one of the highest proportions of venture-capital-backed startups in Switzerland, some of which Basel Area Business & Innovation is proud to have supported during their journey by providing them with access to talent and funding. In total, our directly accelerated companies have raised more than $200 million since 2016. Startups from the Basel Area have ranked highly in the TOP 100 Swiss Startup Award by Venturelab, among other lists and rankings.

In high-tech fields such as biotech, digital health and Industry 4.0, the right funding and coaching from a knowledgeable team is essential. Basel Area Business & Innovation supports and connects startups, intrapreneurs and entrepreneurs with experts, partners, collaborators and funding sources.

Basel Area Business & Innovation provides tailored support for entrepreneurs, startups and SMEs. From founding and funding to growth and scaleup, it mentors and connects founders and others to experts, collaborators and funding sources through events, workshops and acceleration and incubation programs. Its community of national and international innovators, thought leaders, experts and investors is continuously growing, and its services facilitate and nurture innovation to accelerate business growth and create impact.
Visit **innovateinbasel.com** for more information.

contents

STARTUP
GUIDE
BASEL AREA

startups

programs

spaces

experts

founders

schools

investors

Local Ecosystem

[Facts & Figures]
- Basel has Switzerland's highest GDP.
- Basel Area Business & Innovation lists 468 companies as founded or settled in the Basel Area between 2016 and 2020.
- Forty thousand immigrants from 160 different nationalities live in the region.
- The region's key industries are pharmaceuticals, medtech and precision engineering.
- 46% of all research investment in Switzerland happens in the Basel Area's three cantons.
- In the first half of 2019, startups based in Basel saw a nearly 62% increase in investment funding over the previous year, ranking Basel among the top ten investment markets in Europe.
- In 2019, the University of Basel founded the FEMtrepreneurs program, aimed at supporting, funding and promoting women-led businesses.
- The city of Basel has the highest density of museums of any city in Europe.
- Ten of the Basel Area's restaurants are listed in the Michelin Guide.
- Leading investors include the Novartis Venture Fund, Versant Ventures, Roche Venture Fund, and BioMedPartners.

[Notable Startups]
- The region is a hub for big life sciences companies, and the number of startups focusing on biotech and medtech keeps growing, creating a direct collaboration between sectors.
- Several Basel-based companies, including software startup Holo One, a winner of the i4Challenge, and numerous medical and pharmaceutical companies, such as T3 Pharma, are included in the Top 100 Swiss Startups ranking by Venturelab.

Sources: baselarea.swiss, unibas.ch, guide.michelin.com, baselaunch.ch, top100startups.swiss, bfs.admin.ch

[Region] # Basel Area

[Statistics] Area: 1,393 km² (2016)
Population density: 401 per km²
(2019)
Urban Pop.: 558,896 (2019)
GDP: CHF 48.3 billion (2019)
GDP per capita: CHF 346,393
(2018)

STARTUP
GUIDE
BASEL AREA

Basel Area

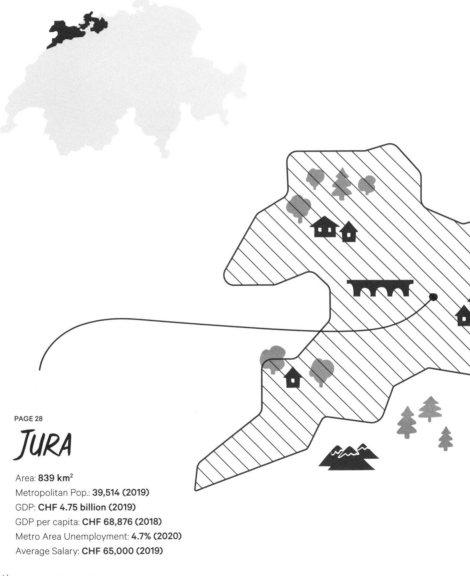

PAGE 28

JURA

Area: **839 km²**
Metropolitan Pop.: **39,514 (2019)**
GDP: **CHF 4.75 billion (2019)**
GDP per capita: **CHF 68,876 (2018)**
Metro Area Unemployment: **4.7% (2020)**
Average Salary: **CHF 65,000 (2019)**

✴ Jura is Switzerland's youngest canton,
only gaining full federal recognition in 1977.

PAGE 24

BASEL-STADT

Area: **36 km²**
Population: **201,971 (2020)**
GDP: **CHF 39.6 billion (2018)**
GDP per capita: **CHF 203,967 (2018)**
Unemployment rate: **3.8% (2020)**
Average Salary: **CHF 80,568 (2018)**

✳ Basler Fasnacht, the largest carnival in
Switzerland, was added to the UNESCO
intangible cultural heritage list in 2017.

PAGE 20

BASEL-LANDSCHAFT

Area: **518 km²**
Metropolitan Pop.: **292,080 (2020)**
GDP: **CHF 21.2 million (2018)**
GDP per capita: **CHF 73,550 (2018)**
Metro Area Unemployment: **2.5%**
Average Salary: **CHF 76,721 (2019)**

✳ Ricola, the herbal candy and cough drop, was
created in Laufen in 1940. The Ricola company
is still based in the area.

N
S

High Quality of Life Meets Entrepreneurial Spirit

Robert Sum / Deputy Head of Economic Development, Kanton Basel-Landschaft

Basel-Landschaft, also referred to as Baselland, is the rural sister canton located next to buzzing Basel-Stadt. Filled with lush forests and picturesque rolling hills, and with a lower cost of living than the city of Basel but the same high quality of infrastructure, the quality of life here is high. Robert Sum, deputy head of economic development at Kanton Basel-Landschaft, acknowledges this is important for both remote workers and entrepreneurs considering the area. A former physicist and entrepreneur who has founded several companies, he started one of his own businesses in a garage within the canton.

Baselland is very friendly to entrepreneurs looking to launch new ventures. "We have a very open administration that's aware of the economic needs of companies," says Robert, adding that the canton strives to support innovative entrepreneurial work. "One of our tasks is to lower the administrative barrier and make it easier to start a company." One example of this is a phone line the canton has created for administrative-related questions called the Welcome Desk. "Depending on the needs of the company, we can connect them to the right people in the administration," Robert explains. The canton administration also provides consulting services for entrepreneurs through business experts such as Business Park Reinach, Laufental and Startup Academy, and has partnered with Basellandschaftliche Kantonalbank on the initiative 100 fürs Baselbiet to provide financing opportunities for new businesses.

Entrepreneurs working in many different industries are based in Baselland, including trades, life sciences, logistics and technology, consumer goods and food production. There are a number of business parks providing workspace across the canton for knowledge workers and life sciences companies, a university hospital and entrepreneurship programs that support community building. All of these things create a fantastic environment for budding entrepreneurs looking for a high quality of life outside of the city. Described by Robert as a place to live, Baselland also doesn't compromise on its connectivity – EuroAirport and Basel city center can be reached in twenty minutes.

[Contact] Email: robert.sum@bl.ch Telephone: +41 61 552 96 89

[Links] Web: baselland.ch LinkedIn: company/kanton-bl Facebook: KantonBL Twitter: @Kanton_BL

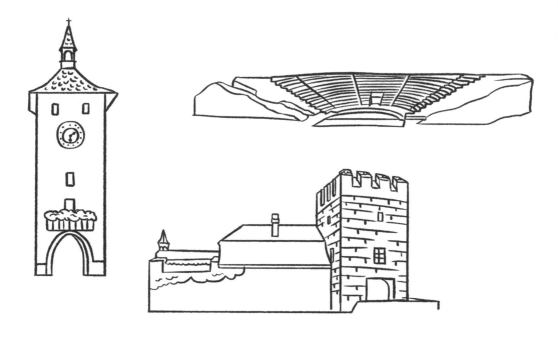

Basel-Landschaft

Right in the heart of Europe you'll find the Swiss canton of Basel-Landschaft, also known as Baselland. An inspirational mix of down-to-earth rural spirit, internationalism and open-mindedness, the canton is linked to the sea and most major cities in Europe through the Rhine harbor, the EuroAirport and various highways and railways. Its central location, highly skilled people and the presence of leading educational institutions make the canton an ideal environment for doing business in life sciences and more.

[Facts & Figures]
- Basel-Landschaft has an attractive tax environment. From 2025, the effective corporate income tax rate will be 13.45% (federal, cantonal and communal level). In addition, special measures including patent box and R&D deduction can reduce the tax burden.
- On average, 49% of the canton's workforce are secondary school graduates, 4% higher than the national average.
- 65% of Baselland citizens choose to embark on professional apprenticeships, creating a highly specialized and skilled workforce even by Swiss standards.
- The canton's location allows it to serve as a gateway to Switzerland from neighboring Germany and France, accepting over 21,000 regular commuting workers who cross the border for work.
- Basel-Landschaft's border location, as well as its proximity to historical industry hubs in Basel-Stadt, makes it an ideal home for international giants including DHL and Bayer.

[Notable Startups]
- Pharmaceuticals and biotechnology company Actelion, founded in 1997, was sold to Johnson & Johnson for CHF 30 billion in 2017. The founders subsequently founded Idorsia to further develop new products.
- Pharmaceutical company Santhera, founded 2004, went public in 2006.
- SKAN developed rapidly to become the leading supplier of cleanroom equipment for the pharmaceutical industry.
- Nanosurf took the canton to Mars with its atomic force microscope, which was used for high-resolution particle analysis on the Mars Odyssey mission.

Sources: bfs.admin.ch, statistik.bl.ch, jobs.ch, economy-bl.ch, baselland.ch

Fertile Ground for Innovative Startups

Samuel Hess / Head of Economic Affairs, Office of Economy and Labour, Kanton Basel-Stadt

Nestled along both sides of the Rhine River and bordered by France and Germany, Basel has everything startups need to start and grow their businesses. Samuel Hess, head of economic affairs at the Office of Economy and Labour, Kanton Basel-Stadt, believes that Basel's central location in Europe and its fantastic transit links, attractive office and lab infrastructure are just a few reasons why. It also has competitive tax rates and access to local and international talent. "Last but not least, you can enjoy an urban lifestyle with affordable housing, trendy bars, restaurants and hotels and the Rhine to relax and recharge your batteries," he says. In addition, the growing startup and innovation community here is bolstered by larger companies, universities, a leading university hospital and a business-friendly government.

The Canton of Basel-Stadt has been actively supporting innovation since 2000. Technologiepark Basel, which celebrated its tenth anniversary in 2021, provides full-service lab and office space with flexible conditions to tech startups. Additionally, acceleration programs such as BaseLaunch and DayOne support biotech and healthcare startups and are operated by Basel Area Business & Innovation and financed in part by the Canton of Basel-Stadt.

Samuel adds that he believes the best global talent pool for the life sciences is available in the region. "Basel is one of the finest locations in the world for biotech, medtech and IT for health entrepreneurs," he says. The large number of life science corporations based in the Canton of Basel-Stadt are interested in collaborating with startups on innovative projects, making it the ideal place for science-focused founders to start their businesses. Additionally, the presence of the University of Basel, the University of Applied Sciences and Arts Northwest Switzerland and the Department of Biosystems Science and Engineering (D-BSSE) of ETH Zurich in Basel foster the development of the lively startup ecosystem by encouraging students to create companies during and after graduation. The intimate yet open-minded environment in Basel creates the perfect conditions for innovation to thrive.

[Contact] Email: samuel.hess@bs.ch Telephone: +41 61 267 85 38 LinkedIn: in/samuel-hess-8bb92a7

[Links] Web: awa.bs.ch LinkedIn: showcase/standortfoerderung-awa-bs Facebook: Rathaus.Basel
Instagram: kantonbaselstadt Twitter: @BaselStadt

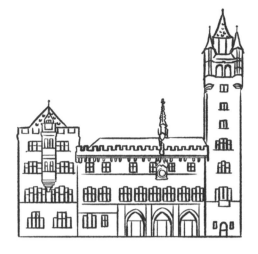

Basel-Stadt

The Canton of Basel-Stadt is a vibrant and diverse cosmopolitan center that serves as the heart of Swiss economic and cultural life. Situated on the French and German borders, the Canton of Basel-Stadt receives around 34,000 workers from both countries each day. Public and private investment options are readily available in fields ranging from finance to biotech, and the city is fertile ground for startups looking to build a future on the international stage while leveraging that famous Swiss-made quality and security.

[Facts & Figures]
- Two of the world's five largest pharmaceutical companies – Novartis and Roche – were founded in the Canton of Basel-Stadt and also have their headquarters and research operations here.
- More than CHF 500 million went into startups in the Canton of Basel-Stadt in 2020, four times more than in the previous record year. Biotech startups were responsible for the sharp increase.
- The region is home to over 700 life sciences companies, with over 32,000 specialists covering the entire life sciences value chain.
- BaselWorld and Art Basel are Basel-based trade fairs with a global presence and appeal.
- The University of Basel is the oldest university in Switzerland. With its numerous research institutes, such as the Center for Innovative Finance, which is unique in Switzerland, it has been an international leader for many years. The University of Applied Sciences and Arts Northwestern Switzerland is the link between research, society and business.

[Notable Startups]
- Several of Switzerland's 100 most innovative and promising startups are located in the Canton of Basel-Stadt.
- Biopharmaceutical company Versameb achieved 49th place in Venturelab's Top 100 Swiss Startups rankings in 2020, and T3 Pharmaceuticals took 52nd place.
- Anaveon and MyCamper are also featured in the ranking.
- In the public vote, Basel-based KetoSwiss and Lyfegen HealthTech were ranked among the top ten.
- Polyneuron, Anaveon and Versameb are based at Technologiepark Basel.

Sources: bs.ch, statistik.bs.ch, basel.com, "Swiss Startup Venture Report 2021" (startupticker.ch), baselarea.swiss, baselworld.com, artbasel.com, top100startups.swiss, baselarea.swiss, "Canton of Jura looking towards robotics" (s-ge.com)

A Balance of Culture, Nature and Industrial Expertise

Lionel Socchi / Head of Economic Promotion, République
et Canton du Jura

Predominantly French-speaking Jura is located next to the French border
and has Baselland to the east and Bern to the south. Paris can be reached
in less than three hours by high-speed train, and the city of Basel is only thirty-five
minutes away by train or car. A mountainous and forested canton, Jura is known
for its beautiful landscapes, numerous hiking trails and high quality of life.
The capital of the canton, Delémont, has a medieval old town that is home
to twelve thousand residents.

Lionel Socchi, head of economic development at République et Canton du Jura
explains that the canton's industrial expertise started with watchmaking and
that this remains one of the main industries today. "Highly specialized suppliers
produce premium components and machines for the worldwide watchmaking
and microtech industry," says Lionel. In addition, Jura has a number of local
and international small and medium-sized businesses in robotics, machinery
and automation, as well as a growing medtech industry.

République et Canton du Jura provides a lot of support for new businesses,
including training for industries with an economic need. Economic Promotion
is the main contact for new businesses, and should be a founder's first port
of call in the canton. "Set up as a one-stop shop, it advises and offers ongoing,
personalized and free-of-charge support," explains Lionel. The Switzerland
Innovation Park Basel Area opened a location in Jura in 2019, and it hosts
innovative startups and projects, as well as a branch office of the Centre Suisse
d'Electronique et de Microtechnique (CSEM). Creapole, a local incubator and
accelerator, further supports early-stage companies along every step of their
development. Nouvelle Entreprise Innovante status provides tax exemptions
and other benefits for new businesses. The growing support for new companies,
good infrastructure to metropolitan business hubs and mix of rural and urban
lifestyle make this canton a great base for budding entrepreneurs.

[Contact]   Email: lionel.socchi@jura.ch Telephone: +41 32 420 51 11

[Links]   Web: jura.ch LinkedIn: company/republique-et-canton-du-jura Facebook: juraoriginalsuisse
Instagram: juraoriginal Twitter: @CantonduJura

Jura

Located on the French border, but with easy train connections to all of Switzerland and its two major airports, Jura is an ideal location for French-speaking entrepreneurs. With the local government proactively investing in startups by offering tax benefits for new companies looking to settle in the area, as well as a history of growth, Jura is quickly becoming one of Switzerland's most economically dynamic locations.

[Facts & Figures]
- Leading industries in Jura are watchmaking, medtech, microtechnology and agriculture.
- Jura is one of the biggest centers of traditional Swiss watchmaking, and is home to Cartier.
- As the youngest member of the Swiss Innovation Park enterprise, the canton has promoted startup development with around CHF 1.6 million invested in its new business-development center.
- Taxation and residence permits are priorities for the local governments, with the financial sector expanding the options, available services and tax cuts for young foreign entrepreneurs.
- Private investors have seen success with incubator sites such as Creapole SA, which in 2020 began hosting forty-five new startups in Delémont.
- The canton provides apprenticeships and investments for women looking to enter watchmaking and microtech.
- Robotics manufacturing and development in Jura has gained national and international attention, with companies including Sonceboz SA moving into the canton and new investments from the Swiss Federal Institute of Technology.

[Notable Startups]
- NextDay.Vision, a cybersecurity startup, won the Basel Area i4 Challenge in 2018 and Tech4Trust award in 2020.
- The healthcare-innovation initiative DayOne has helped local medtech companies expand to Eastern European and US markets.
- Jura hosts two CleanTechAlps member companies: Tripole, a startup incubator; and WaterDiam, a startup focused on clean water production and distribution.

Sources: jura.ch, bfs.admin.ch, "Le Jura, une croissance assez suisse" (letemps.ch), jobs.ch, eco. jura.ch, baselarea.swiss, "Rapport d'activités 2020" (creapole.ch), dayone.swiss, "Panorama des start-ups clean tech" (cleantech-alps.com)

River Rhine

Intro to the Area

The Basel Area is a beautiful and diverse region in the northwest corner of Switzerland that is made up of three cantons: German-speaking Basel-Stadt (Basel City) and Basel-Landschaft (Baselland), as well as the country's youngest canton, French-speaking Jura.

Like Switzerland, the Basel Area is linguistically, culturally and industrially diverse. Basel is the country's third largest city, a cosmopolitan urban area with a long history. Split in the middle by the Rhine River and resting right on the French and German borders, for centuries the city has been a hub for international networking and innovation, and acts as a modern base for diverse global industries like biotech, pharmaceuticals and watchmaking. Basel prides itself on innovation, with one of Switzerland's best success rates for startup funding, high wages and relatively low taxes. As a result of this support, Basel-Stadt has been at the forefront of startup development in central Europe, boasting one of the highest investment amounts per capita. According to the *2021 Swiss Venture Capital Report*, in 2020 Basel posted a new record, receiving over a quarter of all the startup funding in the country, totalling CHF 0.5 billion. But the area isn't just a business hub. It is also home to the renowned University of Basel, one of Europe's oldest educational facilities, and to some of the best museums and cultural institutions in the country. In fact, it's known as the cultural capital of Switzerland. Outside the city, the picturesque cantons of Basel-Landschaft and Jura both offer idyllic lifestyles with their own unique cultures and traditions to explore.

Before You Come

Switzerland is home to an international workforce but getting a work permit isn't always easy, so it's important to have your documents in order. The best places to start are the cantons' websites: **bs.ch** for Basel-Stadt, **baselland.ch** for Baselland and **jura.ch** for Jura. Also consult the Swiss Secretariat for Migration (SEM) website (**sem.admin.ch**) for information and resources to help plan your move. Whichever canton you move to, renting can be complex when you're new, so book temporary accommodation first to allow you to get organized. Note that Swiss power sockets are different from the European standard. Most work interchangeably, but it's best to bring adapters just in case. Summers in Basel are mild, and winters are damp and cold. Bring essential warm clothing with you, as it can be expensive in Switzerland. In general, be prepared to spend some money: Switzerland may have low taxes, but the cost of living is one of the highest in Europe.

Visas and Work Permits

Swiss citizens are prioritized for positions and their hiring is incentivized by both the local and federal governments. EU/EFTA citizens can spend up to three months in the country looking for a job on a tourist visa, which can be prolonged to a year with a short-term permit. Register with a regional employment center, which can help you with changing permits. Non-EU/EFTA citizens must apply for a visa before entering the country. The permit types are identified by letters: L permits are for short-term residence, and B permits are standard residence permits that can be renewed or eventually turned into a C permit, which is for longer-term settlement. Only approximately 8,500 temporary B and L permits are issued each year, which means that it can be tough to get a visa if you're not in a prioritized field like STEM, or lack the educational or language skills these job quotas favor. You should check your canton's specific employment and permit requirements on its website, and also consult the SEM site for more details. If you're having a hard time getting a visa that allows you to work, you might be able to join the thousands of workers who commute to the region from France and Germany. Freelance visas are more accessible in these two countries, allowing for a dynamic transnational lifestyle.

See **Important Government Offices** page **200**

Basel Town Hall

Kunstmuseum

Cultural Differences

The Swiss are famous for their punctuality, attention to detail and orderliness, and these qualities are apparent both in working culture and social life. Newcomers might face some culture shock, as everything from waste disposal to home noise levels is highly regulated. You'll also notice cultural differences in architecture, food and lifestyle between cantons, especially between the different linguistic regions. This cantonal diversity is one of the most interesting parts of living in Switzerland. But wherever you live, it is essential to be an active member of the community and stay up to date with what's going on in your area. You will soon notice that your neighbors are always voting on referendums, and this direct democracy is something that can impact you directly as an immigrant. If you ultimately decide to apply for citizenship after a few years, in some cantons your neighbors might be voting to approve your application, so being a good neighbor could be an investment in your future.

Cost of Living

While the Basel Area has a lower cost of living than other Swiss metropolitan areas, living in Switzerland is still expensive. Rent, which generally does not include utilities, ranges between CHF 1,500 and 2,000 per month for a one-bedroom in Basel city center, with rates dropping only slightly in the suburbs. Jura and Baselland have more affordable housing options. Mandatory health insurance starts around CHF 300 per month for a basic plan and can go well into the thousands depending on your deductible and family size. Full-time childcare costs CHF 60–CHF 150 per day. If you plan on using public transport regularly, get the SBB Half Fare Travelcard, which reduces the cost of tickets by half, and costs CHF 185 per year. Budget CHF 550–CHF 750 per month for food and utilities for one person. All told, the average cost of living for a single adult before rent starts at around CHF 1,500. In general, it's best to plan on things costing more than elsewhere in Europe.

Messe Basel New Hall

Accommodation

Like almost everything in Switzerland, accommodation rules vary by canton. In any canton, it's crucial to have an application letter detailing your salary, profession and marital and legal status. Some real estate sites, such as **homegate.ch**, can help you put this together. Your landlord may require you to provide an extract from the debt-collection register, demonstrating whether you have ever been pursued by debt collectors. You might also be required to have a Swiss bank account and pay three months' rent in advance. Most Swiss apartments don't come furnished, but they often have laundry facilities in the basement of the building. Community is paramount, so be aware of your building's rules, like where to purchase your mail nameplate, designated smoking areas and quiet hours. The Federal Office of Housing (BWO) website (**bwo.admin.ch**) and the Swiss Authorities guides at **ch.ch** have more details.

See **Accommodation** page **199**

Insurance

Insurance is an essential part of life in Switzerland, as every resident is legally required to purchase a basic health insurance plan. Visit **bag.admin.ch** for the requirements and a list of authorized health insurers. Make sure that you fully understand your plan's coverage, as many basic plans do not cover accident-related injuries or dental health. Policies can also be provided through an employer. Other kinds of insurance, such as third-party liability for tenants, vary between cantons, so be sure to check the requirements on your canton's website. Many landlords also ask for contents insurance as a condition for renting. Auto insurance is mandatory if you own any motorized vehicle, but double check your coverage details as many basic plans do not cover damages to your vehicle or passengers. Various special plans are also available for any situation in Swiss life, including alpine climbing and skiing.

See **Insurance Companies** page **200**

Basel Minster

Starting a Company

The Basel Area is on track to become one of the biggest startup hubs in central Europe, and the region has taken significant steps to make starting a business easier. In some cases, you can even set up a business entirely online through the **easygov.swiss** website. However, if you don't have Swiss/EU/EFTA citizenship or permanent residency, your canton must first authorize you to open a business. This involves submitting a very detailed business plan to the local authorities and proving that the company will have a long-lasting, positive impact on the community. Once your project is approved, you will be granted a short-term permit to start your business. Each canton has its own business and entrepreneurial support resources and contacts that can be accessed via its website. For example, Jura has streamlined the process for startups with its Economic Promotion division (**eco.Jura.ch**). This is a one-stop shop where you can get help with everything from the legal requirements to infrastructure and even hiring qualified locals. Agencies including Basel Area Business & Innovation (**baselarea.swiss**) can help you get set up or move an existing business to the area, but self-employment and freelancing still have some legal limitations if you're not Swiss or an EU/EFTA national. All the information and checklists you need can be found at **kmu.admin.ch** or your canton's business resources page. You can also use a specialist service like **lexpat.ch** to help start your company.

See **Programs** page **68**

Opening a Bank Account

The Swiss are known for international banking, and financial institutions are everywhere. Some banks might require you to have a B or C permit to open an account, but PostFinance, the national postal service bank, is legally required to provide banking options to every resident. Credit Suisse and UBS are the two biggest banks in the country and have extensive English-language customer service and international client solutions, making them reliable options. Every canton also has its own *Kantonalbank*, which often have special offers for local startups, so check your specific Kantonalbank's site. In most cases, banking is still a personal affair, so you'll need to go to a branch to finalize your account. Past issues of tax evasion and privacy breaches can make the application process harder for people from specific nationalities. Depending on your citizenship, additional documentation might be needed to open a bank account, and different fees and regulations may apply. In daily life, cash is still important in most of the country, but most places also accept cards.

See **Banks** page **199**

Helvetia auf Reisen

Taxes

Swiss taxes are much lower than in the rest of Europe, and they are collected on a federal, cantonal and local basis. This means that there are advantages to living in different cantons and municipalities — Baselland and Jura will almost certainly be cheaper than Basel-Stadt. Newcomers who do not hold a C permit have their taxes deducted automatically from their salaries, as long as they do not exceed CHF 120,000 per year. This is also the case for B permit holders for the first five years of living in Switzerland. If you commute into Switzerland from another country, you must submit proof of residence to demonstrate that your income is being taxed elsewhere. To become familiar with the dos and don'ts, it's advised to use a local tax preparation service that is experienced with expats and international entrepreneurs, especially if you're not from the EU/EFTA. BC-IT (**bc-it.ch**) and klein TREUHAND (**kleintreuhand.ch**) are two options. US citizens have yet another layer of complexity, and should consider specialist services like AIT Services (**americanincometax.com**).

See **Financial Services** page **200**

Phone and Internet

The three leading telecom providers are Swisscom, Salt and Sunrise, which all offer simple plans and bundles for personal, household and business use. Coverage and speed are excellent throughout the country, even in rural areas. Be sure to check your contract carefully before committing, as telecom contracts in Switzerland can be costly and difficult to get out of. If you are just settling in, consider using a prepaid SIM card/phone from Migros or Swiss Post. This will give you a better idea of how much data you will eventually need, with the flexibility to change providers before you're locked into a 12- or 24-month minimum contract. Because the Basel Area is so close to France and Germany, you may also want to add European coverage to your plan to avoid roaming charges.

Getting Around

The Swiss public transport system is one of the best in the world, and with SBB (**sbb.ch**), PostAuto (**postauto.ch**) and regional networks you can get anywhere in the country fairly easily. Basel is very walkable and bike-friendly, and the vast network of trams and buses can take you all over the city and across the border. The region is also a transport hub, and you'll find that regional connections using BVB (**bvb.ch**) in Basel-Stadt and TNW (**tnw.ch**) in Baselland are quick and frequent. Both local and national transportation providers accept a variety of discounts, including the Half-Fare Travelcard, which gives you half off most tickets in Switzerland.

Street view, Basel-Stadt

The SBB app is indispensable, featuring live timetables and allowing route planning and fare purchase. Just don't be tempted to abuse the ticket honor system — if you are found without a ticket, there's a significant fine. Drivers will find that Swiss roads are in excellent condition, but be careful to follow the strict speed limit.

Learning the Language

Switzerland has four official languages: German, French, Italian and Romansh. Multilingualism is a fact of life and it's quite common to start a conversation with a new person by talking about language. In Basel-Stadt and Baselland, the *Baseldytsch* dialect of Swiss German is spoken, but Standard German is taught in all schools and the Swiss are used to switching. In Jura, French is spoken. The city of Basel is very international, so you'll have no problem finding English speakers, but language is a critical component for successful integration, so it's important to make an effort if you're planning to stay. Depending on your permit level and canton, you may actually need to prove some proficiency in your canton's primary language. The SEM website has a comprehensive list of requirements, and there are plenty of language schools in the region to help, including Berlitz (**berlitz.com/en-ch**) and Inlingua (**inlingua-basel.ch**).

See **Language Schools** page **200**

Meeting People

The Basel Area is culturally rich and dynamic, with a full calendar of seasonal events in addition to the plentiful museums. From riverfront parties in the summer and the world-famous Christmas market, to the Basel Tattoo drum festival and the largest carnival in Switzerland, there's something for everyone. Messe Basel is the largest exhibition centre in Switzerland, and its regular events, including world-renowned Art Basel, are great opportunities for socializing and networking. For sports, there's the local football team, FC Basel. If you are more of an outdoorsy type, there's great hiking and climbing in Jura, and in Baselland the Roman ruins of Augusta Raurica make an interesting place to explore. World-class skiing is also only a short train ride away. Basel Area is also great for foodies, as a place where French, German, and Italian haute cuisine meet Swiss quality. Check out the Basel page on **meetup.com** to find like-minded people and events.

start

ups

[Name]

Alentis Therapeutics

[Elevator Pitch]

"We're a small team developing new cutting-edge treatments for fibrotic disease and associated cancers."

[The Story]

Alentis Therapeutics began its journey in the laboratory of Dr. Thomas Baumert, a professor at the University of Strasbourg and the French National Institute of Health. While studying the molecular pathogenesis of hepatitis B and C infections, Thomas realized that the protein claudin-1 (CLDN1), which plays a key role in hepatitis, is also involved in fibrotic diseases, including liver and kidney disease, and their related cancers. Together, fibrotic disorders are responsible for an estimated 45 percent of deaths in the US and Europe alone, and few effective treatments are currently available. With this in mind, Thomas began working on new therapies that would specifically target CLDN1.

In late 2017, Thomas took his research to the BaseLaunch program. The incubator provided initial funding and helped to build the Alentis team from scratch, connecting the founder with Basel-based pharma-business veterans who could help turn his ideas into a viable product. In 2019, the company officially launched after completing a Series A financing round led by venture capital firms from Switzerland, France and Germany. In 2020, CEO Roberto Iacone, previously with healthcare giant Roche, joined the team. After completing preclinical studies and safety trials, Alentis raised additional Series B financing in June 2021. The company is preparing to conduct clinical trials and aims to launch a product on the market by 2026.

[Funding History]

External   Grants

Alentis was initially funded by a CHF 250,000 grant from BaseLaunch in 2017, and in 2019 it received CHF 12.5 million in Series A funding. June 2021 saw the completion of a Series B round totalling CHF 60 million led by Morningside Venture Investments in conjunction with Jeito Capital and previous Series A investors.

[Milestones]

- Launching Alentis Therapeutics in April 2019.
- Bringing on CEO Roberto Iacone in 2020.
- Completing studies on primates that indicated our product could be safely used on human patients.
- Receiving CHF 60 million in Series B financing.

[Links]   Web: **alentis.ch** LinkedIn: **company/alentis-therapeutics**

[Name] # ARTIDIS

[Elevator Pitch] *"Our vision is to change the standard of care in tissue analysis. Our nanotechnology platform combines tissue-biopsy analysis with robust patient-data analytics and can be applied to any living tissue or material, with a broad range of clinical and R & D applications."*

[The Story] The idea for ARTIDIS came about when CEO Dr. Marija Plodinec and CMO Dr. Marko Loparic were PhD students at the University of Basel, where they were working on atomic force microscopy. Realizing the technology had applications for biological samples, they assembled a team to build a medical-device prototype. After filing for a patent through the university's technology transfer office, they obtained R&D grants to build and test their first prototypes in a clinical setting. In 2016, they ran a clinical validation study in oncology to obtain proof of concept before raising funds to take it to the next level. Today, ARTIDIS has a US office and is collaborating with one of the world's largest medical centers, Texas Medical Center, as well as institutions in Europe, to begin large-scale clinical trials to gain regulatory approval and take the technology to market.

In contrast to standard diagnostic tests, the ARTIDIS device detects the physical properties of tissue. It can quickly distinguish healthy cells from tumor cells at the patient's bedside. The measurements obtained can be used to assess response to treatments like radiotherapy or to get an indication of the development of resistance, allowing for treatment decisions to be taken in real time.

[Funding History]

Seed External Grants

ARTIDIS has obtained two R&D grants from Innosuisse, totaling over CHF 2 million. Three seed rounds and a Series A round raised CHF 25 million in total. A Series B round is planned to raise CHF 20 million.

[Milestones]

- Founding ARTIDIS on the back of our Nature Nanotechnology cover feature, and being cited over seven hundred times.

- Having eight global patent families granted or pending approval.

- Recruiting 545 patients to our first clinical validation study and achieving proof of concept.

- Establishing strategic collaborations with the Texas Medical Center and other leading medical centers in the US and EU.

[Links] Web: **artidis.com** LinkedIn: **company/artidis** Twitter: **@artidis_ag**

[Name] # InnoSpina

[Elevator Pitch] *"We leverage 3D printing to design and develop innovative spinal implants and unique surgical guiding instruments to treat chronic back pain. Our technique significantly reduces the risks of surgery and cuts operating times from two hours to under thirty minutes."*

[The Story] InnoSpina was cofounded in 2017 by renowned spinal surgeon Dr. Jacques Samani, entrepreneurial engineer Gwenael Hannema and Nicole Beuchat, cofounder of additive manufacturing company 3D Precision. Given the complexities of spinal surgery, it took a lot of trial and error before a workable implant prototype was achieved in 2019. What sets InnoSpina's products apart from competitors are the reduced costs and risks and greater ease of use. "It's super intuitive," says Gwenael. "The implant just glides into position while protecting the spinal cord at all times."

All three cofounders initially worked other jobs to finance the project before Gwenael became full-time CEO in 2020. He successfully secured investment to accelerate product development, and the first implant is on track to hit the market in 2024. InnoSpina's implants have already piqued the interest of spinal surgeons, and some have signed letters of intent. The team now includes five full-time engineers working on R&D, and InnoSpina is looking to attract experienced talent to complement its executive management and advisory board. The company also benefits from the input of experienced medtech advisors through the Basel DayOne accelerator program. InnoSpina's goals include obtaining medical certification, growing its patent portfolio and preparing for a seed round.

[Funding History]

Bootstrap   Pre-Seed   Grants

InnoSpina was bootstrapped before obtaining two non-dilutive R&D grants totaling CHF 1.3 million from Innosuisse (Swiss Agency for Innovation Promotion) and the Jura Economic Promotion agency in 2020. It has also received a convertible loan of CHF 50,000 from Venture Kick.

[Milestones]

- Validating our first prototype implant and instrument in specimens and achieving a surgery time of under thirty minutes.

- Filing our patent applications.

- Securing CHF 1.3 million in non-dilutive funding for two R&D projects.

- Getting our first signed letters of intent from key opinion leaders and spinal surgeons.

[Links] Web: **innospina.com** LinkedIn: **company/innospina**

[Name] # MyCamper

[Elevator Pitch] *"Think of us as the Airbnb for campers in Switzerland – we connect people who own camping vehicles with people who want to rent them, helping conserve fixed costs and resources."*

[The Story] Carsharing companies often point out how little time the average car actually spends on the road – but for camper vehicles, it's even less. This realization is what brought MyCamper's trio of cofounders together in 2015, with the goal of creating a sharing platform that would benefit camper owners and renters alike. An early challenge for the startup was finding an insurance partner. As the carsharing concept is still so new, many companies were reluctant to get on board. From a simple site with fewer than a dozen users, the founders worked to encourage growth on both the supply and demand side of the equation – increasing marketing to would-be renters when more campers were available, and cutting it off when the numbers leveled out. "That's the one thing that's really important to us – that the two sides are growing at the same pace," explains cofounder Mirjam Affolter.

As the company's user base grew, the founders hunted for funding. After completing their first round of financing, they landed a coveted spot on the first season of *Die Höhle der Löwen*, Switzerland's version of the show *Shark Tank*, which generated not only more funds, but a good deal of publicity as well. Today, the platform boasts nearly two thousand available vehicles, and a potential expansion into Scandinavia is on the horizon.

[Funding History]

Bootstrap   Angel   External

The team began with bootstrapping, before raising a round of almost $300,000 from angel investors in 2018. The appearance on *Die Höhle der Löwen* netted the company another $300,000, followed by another $150,000 investment from the network of one of the show's investors. In 2020, MyCamper completed a pre–Series A financing round of about $1 million.

[Milestones]

- Partnering with an insurance company so that our users would be more easily covered.
- Appearing on the show *Die Höhle der Löwen*.
- Reaching one thousand camping vehicles on our platform.
- Becoming partners with the official Swiss touring club.

[Links] Web: **mycamper.ch** Facebook: **mycamper.ch** Instagram: **mycamper.ch** Twitter: **@myCamper_CH**

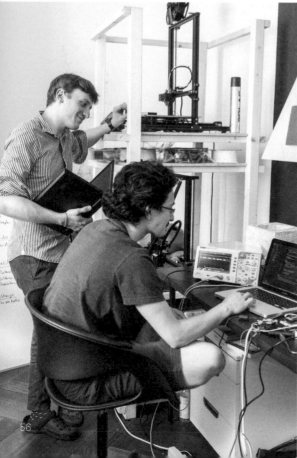

[Name] # Mycrobez

[Elevator Pitch] *"We use mushrooms and agricultural waste to make a compostable alternative to polystyrene packaging. It's affordable, durable, lightweight and breaks down in nature in less than ninety days, so recovered material can be used for fertilizer."*

[The Story] Mycrobez cofounders Mosas Pilscheur, Jonas Staub and Moritz Schiller were still in high school when they realized they had a commercial opportunity. After Jonas won an innovation award for 3D printing mycelium (mushroom) cells, they started researching the applications of mushrooms using grow-your-own kits to obtain material for testing. On entering the Swiss Student Sustainability Challenge and Swiss Student Startup Challenge in 2019, market analyses revealed the commercial applications for biodegradable packaging. After winning both challenges, the cofounders secured a place in the Impact Hub Basel incubator program, invested their prize money in a lab and founded Mycrobez. While mycelium composites aren't new, the startup is working to achieve automation of a costly manual process and has designed a circular production model with two upcycling stages.

After months of R&D, in 2020 Mycrobez achieved its first prototype and sale, to a jewelry brand. Moritz and Mosas manage the business side while Jonas handles R&D, assisted by the company's first employees. Mycrobez is working on refining its production process and product for launch in Switzerland in 2023 and Germany and Austria in 2024. Pilot projects with Swiss OEMs and exporters are underway.

[Funding History]

Pre-Seed   Grants

Mycrobez started in 2019 with a CHF 20,000 loan from Mosas' father and CHF 10,000 in challenge prize money. In 2020, the company closed a pre-seed round for CHF 250,000 and received CHF 15,000 for R&D from Innosuisse. Private foundations have also contributed grants totaling CHF 45,000.

[Milestones]

- Achieving our minimum viable product.
- Closing our pre-seed financing round.
- Taking on our first employees.
- Initiating discussions with our first strategic partners.

[Links]   Web: **mycrobez.ch** LinkedIn: **company/mycrobez** Instagram: **mycrobez**

[Name] # NextDay.Vision

[Elevator Pitch] *"We simplify cyber security, making it easier for organizations to take ownership of their own security processes. Through a range of services, software and management solutions, we help to make our customers' lives easier when it comes to IT security."*

[The Story] Founded in 2017 by Philippe Kapfer and Sabrina Gessier, NextDay.Vision aims to make cyber security easier to understand and more accessible to businesses. Prior to setting up the company, Philippe worked for a range of IT companies and found that they were not open to simplifying processes for the user. He was frustrated by the lack of focus on the customer and end user, and wanted to change this. After completing a master's and publishing a book on hacking and countermeasures, Philippe started NextDay.Vision with Sabrina, a former teacher with a background in marketing and communication.

From providing "no-password" authentication to comprehensive IT security audits, NextDay.Vision is committed to educating leadership teams on how to ensure cyber security remains a priority and is not just the responsibility of the IT team. Philippe says, "We make cyber security simple so that businesses can rest assured that their security systems are fully integrated and that they can manage these systems in an easy way." NextDay.Vision also develops built-in security systems. For example, NextDay.Vision can help an organization building an app to create the security or authentication part of the app. In the next five years, NextDay.Vision's founders hope to drive industry change towards a "no-password" model that moves away from the cloud with improved localized security measures. The company's long-term ambition is to expand across Europe.

[Funding History]

Bootstrap   Pre-Seed   Seed

NextDay.Vision was initially funded by its founders. In 2019, it received investment from Netmanage SA, a Swiss-based IT company. It is seeking outside investment from private equity funds with a view to expand internationally.

[Milestones]

- Winning the Tech4Trust accelerator from the EPFL Innovation Park.
- Being recognized as a New Innovative Company in the Canton of Jura.
- Taking part in the I-Moutier incubator and winning the I4 Challenge in 2018.
- Pioneering simpler internet security and leading the industry with "no-password" software.

[Links] Web: **nextday.vision** LinkedIn: **company/nextday-vision** Twitter: **@nextday_vision**

125 mg/dL

Nutrix

[Name]

[Elevator Pitch]

"We develop sensors for digital health monitoring based on biomarkers in saliva. The core development focuses on noninvasive glucose-monitoring sensors, but we're also expanding to monitoring the stress hormone cortisol."

[The Story]

Nutrix started in 2019, when CEO Maria Hahn met her cofounder and CDO Nikhil Singh at an MIT boot camp. The concept behind Nutrix was to use technology for preventive health. Maria says that the idea came up during a lunch break, when one of her colleagues asked "Why don't we put a sensor on the tooth?" This idea was later presented at Web Summit 2019, where the team won the PITCH competition.

In 2020, Nutrix received two grants, including one from the Chilean government, that allowed it to build a prototype and do the first tests. Given the COVID-19 pandemic, the cofounders decided that before marketing the tooth sensor, it would be a good idea to design and get its core diagnostic device to market. The product, called gSense, is a noninvasive and pain-free device that monitors the levels of glucose in saliva and sends the data to a mobile app. The company is also developing a sensor to monitor the hormone cortisol, which will help users to keep track of stress levels. In 2021, Nutrix joined a healthtech program at Silicon Valley–based Plug and Play, which will allow the team to gain more knowledge about the US market. The company is growing, and the current team of three has plans to expand to include AI engineers, among others.

[Funding History]

Seed   Grants

Nutrix has received a total of $100,000 in grants. These include a grant from Venture Kick, a Swiss organization for startups, and a grant from Start-Up Chile, backed by the Chilean government.

[Milestones]

- Winning the Web Summit PITCH Competition in 2019.
- Receiving grants from Venture Kick and Start-Up Chile.
- Becoming a part of Start-Up Chile's accelerator program.
- Joining the Plug and Play healthtech program in 2021.

[Links]

Web: **nutrix.tech** LinkedIn: **company/nutrix-tech** Facebook: **gSense.club**
Instagram: **gSenseclub** Twitter: **@NutrixTech**

Synendos Therapeutics

[Name]

[Elevator Pitch]
"We develop first-in-class endocannabinoid modulators to restore natural functioning of the brain in central nervous system disorders."

[The Story] Synendos Therapeutics' roots can be traced back to when cofounder Dr. Andrea Chicca was working at the University of Bern. "The goal of our research was to translate innovative findings into new pharmacotherapies to tackle unmet needs in human medicine," he explains. This idea eventually came to fruition after several years of thorough research, when new compounds that could be helpful in treating diseases were finally developed. Though the idea at that time was not to spin out the project, the move from academia to a business was straightforward thanks to Switzerland and Basel's vibrant startup ecosystem.

Following a spinning-out phase of two years, from 2017 to 2019, Synendos Therapeutics was eventually founded in April 2019. The startup is devoted to developing safe and effective therapies for neuropsychiatric disorders. In particular, Synendos develops a new class of small molecules aimed at restoring the natural functioning of the brain by targeting the master regulator of brain neurotransmission – the endocannabinoid system. This approach looks very promising for treating a wide range of central nervous system disorders.

[Funding History]

External   Grants

In total, Synendos has received €26 million in funding. €22 million was secured in 2020/21 with a Series A financing round. In addition, the company has been supported with €1.2 million from grants, accelerators and other programs including EU, Innosuisse, BaseLaunch, Venture Kick and InnoBooster (Gebert Rüf Stiftung), and €2.8 million from Eurostars.

[Milestones]

- Receiving €26 million in funding.
- Selecting the right candidates for preclinical and clinical development.
- Ensuring robust patent protection.
- Developing strong proof of concept in a preclinical context to show that the mode of action works.

[Links] Web: **synendos.com** LinkedIn: **company/synendos** Twitter: **@synendos**

TOLREMO

[Name]

[Elevator Pitch]

"We develop novel therapies that can be combined with existing cancer drugs to prevent resistance development and that extend the lives of cancer patients. We make sure the right patient is treated with the right drug at the right time."

[The Story]

TOLREMO therapeutics AG is a privately held Swiss biotechnology company that was formed in 2017. Following her PhD at the Eidgenössische Technische Hochschule Zürich (ETH) and under the guidance of Wilhelm Krek, CEO Stefanie Flückiger-Mangual established the company with four other cofounders. With extensive expertise in the area of non-mutational drug resistance, the company's vision is to create long-lasting cancer therapies. Through its R&D program, the company has developed resistance-preventing companion therapies that increase the benefits of cancer drugs and extend patients' lives. Stefanie says, "Most cancer therapies work for around a year or so and then the tumors become resistant and they grow back. Often, the reason why people lose their lives is not due to a lack of available drugs but to a lack of durable responses to their treatment. We want to use our research to change this."

Since 2017, the company has grown to twelve people and developed a novel drug candidate that is ready to be taken to clinics in 2022. Stefanie says, "Our drug-resistance platform has the potential to create a new wave of molecules that break resistance and work as add-on therapies that meaningfully extend the lives of cancer patients."

[Funding History]

Angel   Seed   External

In its first six months, TOLREMO secured CHF 2.5 million through experienced private biotech investors and a Swiss bank. A year later, it received backing from venture capitalists and raised CHF 9 million through Series A funding, which was later extended to CHF 13.5 million.

[Milestones]

- Winning the Swiss Innovation Challenge in 2019.

- Building a patent portfolio, including novel drug-resistance preventing chemical substances.

- Identifying a novel modulator of cancer-drug resistance whose inhibition prevents the emergence of drug resistance.

- Establishing an operational team, a strong investor base and the nomination of a clinical development candidate in 2021.

[Links]   Web: **tolremo.com** LinkedIn: **company/tolremo-therapeutics**

[Name]
Typewise

[Elevator Pitch]

"We make life easier with one-of-a-kind products that are shaping human–machine interaction. With our free Typewise app, we take the pain out of typing. Users can type faster, with four times fewer typos and safe in the knowledge their privacy is secure."

[The Story]

Founded by David Eberle and Janis Berneeker in 2015, Typewise is changing the way humans and machines interact, and in the process solving some of the most tedious problems of using technology. In the Typewise app, the company has created a next-generation smartphone keyboard that takes the pain out of typing. Following intensive research, it redesigned and supercharged the old QWERTY keyboard with patented autocorrect AI and honeycomb-shaped keys. Customers can type faster, with improved accuracy and in multiple languages. The app learns the user's language choices and keeps their typing history and privacy secure. David says, "We want to create products that are easier to use, that are intuitive and that continually adapt to the users' needs and in turn help people to be more productive."

David and Janis met in high school and took rather different career paths: David has built a career in strategy, while Janis has a background in data science. In 2015, Janis approached David with the idea of rethinking the keyboard. Following a successful crowdfunding campaign and an appearance on the TV show *Die Höhle der Löwen* that resulted in the company receiving funding, the app has now been downloaded over one million times. Typewise has ambitions to grow and expand the business to help every household with products that take the hassle out of using technology.

[Funding History]

Bootstrap   Pre-Seed   Seed

In 2015, David and Janis started a successful Kickstarter campaign. In 2019, they launched the app and received $400,000 from local federal sources for R&D. The following year, Typewise raised $1 million from a variety of business angels, and it is currently securing further funding.

[Milestones]

- Launching the app in December 2019 and growing the user base at 15 percent per month.

- Starting a research partnership with ETH Zurich to research and develop our AI technology.

- Securing funding of $1 million in July 2020, and participating in *Die Höhle der Löwen*.

- Achieving one million downloads and installations of our app.

[Links]   Web: **typewise.app**   LinkedIn: **company/typewise**   Twitter: **@typewise_app**

rams

- **Have something to offer the Basel area.**
  If you're not already based here, we want to know how you'll contribute to the region. Ideally, you'll have proof of your commitment to relocate.

- **Look towards the future.**
  We're looking for innovation, not business as usual.

- **Demonstrate proof of concept.**
  You don't need to have completely developed your product yet, but you need to show us you're serious. For apps, that means a prototype. For life sciences startups, it means preliminary studies or doctor testimonies.

- **Know what you're doing.**
  We don't want to see pitch decks – we want a well-thought-out, elaborate business plan.

[Name]
100 fürs Baselbiet

[Elevator Pitch]
"Led by Swiss bank BLKB, our limited-time initiative provides low-interest loans, mentoring and other support to startups and SMEs that generate value in the Basel Area."

[Sector]
Sector-agnostic

[Description]
In November 2019, BLKB, the University of Applied Sciences and Arts Northwestern Switzerland and the economic development department of Kanton Basel-Landschaft launched an ambitious economic-development plan for Basel and its environs. Together, they would select, finance and support a total of one hundred startups and SMEs, under the condition that they create value in the area. This could mean being headquartered in the Basel region, being willing to relocate to the area, or basing a significant part of operations there.

All companies chosen for 100 fürs Baselbiet receive a three-year low-interest loan in the range of CHF 100,000–CHF 500,000, along with access to coaching and mentoring from a network of experts and assistance in finding suitable sites. The first thirty participants also receive the option of a free month at the 5th Floor coworking space. The program has close ties to the local accelerator inQbator, which is also backed by BLKB. 100 fürs Baselbiet participants can access inQbator's mentor network and other services, while inQbator participants receive advice on how best to secure the 100 fürs Baselbiet funding.

Approximately one-quarter of the one hundred startups have already been selected. As might be expected in Basel, many of them come from the life sciences field – but not all. Participants include Kitro, which is developing technology to aid in food-waste reduction, custom bike-frame company ACR8 and sustainable craft brewery Birtel. There is no set time frame for choosing the remainder of the participants. The program accepts new applications on a quarterly basis, and the most promising are reviewed by an advisory board, which makes the final selection.

[Apply to]
100fuersbb.ch/en/register

[Links]
Web: **100fuersbb.ch** LinkedIn: **company/blkb** Instagram: **blkb_ch**

- **Have a breakthrough innovation.**
  We're looking for exceptional science that can
  form the basis of a new biotech venture.

- **Work in therapeutics.**
  We're interested in therapies for any application,
  in any form. If your project involves medical
  devices, ehealth or diagnostics, check out
  the DayOne accelerator.

- **Have good initial data.**
  Ideally, you've done preliminary in-vivo studies
  and have compelling data to back up your great
  idea. However, in rare cases, we've backed
  companies based only on in-vitro data or earlier.

- **Be at the beginning of your journey.**
  Our companies can be at any stage – from pre-seed
  to seed, or even earlier – but if you've already raised
  significant financing and are well established, we're
  probably not the best fit.

- **Make a strong commitment.**
  We're looking for founders who are willing
  and able to take their project all the way.

[Name] # BaseLaunch

[Elevator Pitch] *"We partner with scientists and entrepreneurs to help launch and grow biotech companies developing cutting-edge therapeutics."*

[Sector] **Biotech, pharmaceutical**

[Description] Pick a hot new therapeutics startup in the Basel region, and there's a good chance it got its start with BaseLaunch. Since early 2018, the incubator and accelerator – operated by Basel Area Business & Innovation – has helped over a dozen founders turn innovative ideas into viable companies. You don't need to be an established startup to apply; in fact, the majority of companies in BaseLaunch's portfolio started off as a promising research project in a university lab, spearheaded by a single professor, post-doc scientist or group leader. The incubator provides successful projects with direct convertible loan funding of up to $500,000, connects them with its network, and helps build out the companies from scratch – by complementing their academic team with a biopharma-savvy chair, for example.

At the beginning, BaseLauch companies often stay within their university research labs. While they don't initially need to be based in Basel, founders are required to formally incorporate or legally register in the region. As they grow and raise further capital, many BaseLaunch ventures take advantage of the incubator's partnership with the Technologiepark Basel and the Switzerland Innovation Park Basel Area and establish their first independent labs or offices out of one of those spaces.

The incubator has no set time frame or conditions. Instead, BaseLaunch is committed to doing whatever it takes, for however long is needed, to help its companies succeed, with the ultimate goal of receiving significant follow-on investment. Typically, that takes the form of Series A financing, but it could also be a collaboration with a pharma corporation – whatever puts the company on solid ground. Successful graduates of BaseLaunch include Alentis Therapeutics, which is developing breakthrough treatments for fibrotic diseases, and Synendos, which specializes in therapies for neuropsychiatric diseases. Since BaseLaunch supported its first ventures in 2018, its portfolio has grown to fifteen companies, which have collectively raised over $270 million in venture financing to date.

[Apply to] **baselaunch.ch/apply**

[Links] Web: **baselaunch.ch** LinkedIn: **company/baselaunch** Twitter: **@BaseLaunch**

 - Know your vision and mission.
  Think about the purpose of the company.
  Why should it exist, and what does it do for
  its stakeholders and customers?

- Have a USP.
  Think about your product or service and what
  differentiates it from competitors.

- Think about the market.
  Who are your customers? Try to quantify your
  market as best as you can.

- Marketing is key.
  Think about how you will reach potential customers.

- Consider all other aspects of setting up a business.
  This includes your team, the legal form of your
  company, the location, finances and risk analysis,
  among others.

[Name] # Business Park Oberbaselbiet | Laufental | Thierstein

[Elevator Pitch] *"We offer free consultation and personal coaching for startups."*

[Sector] **Sector-agnostic**

[Description] Established in 2006, Business Park Oberbaselbiet | Laufental | Thierstein aims to promote and facilitate startups by advising and supporting new businesses through various activities. "The foundation was established because we wanted to strengthen entrepreneurship in the region and, until then, there was no organization that supported young entrepreneurs in their process," says president Marc Scherrer. Entrepreneurs can access a consultation and coaching program at locations in Zwingen and Liestal. The program is aimed at anyone with a business idea who would like to discuss their concept and have it evaluated in a confidential setting by an experienced coach. The initiative also caters to those looking to take over an existing company in the form of a succession plan. Successful applicants will go through two phases: an initial consultation and business plan coaching.

The program starts with phase one, which consists of an initial interview. In the initial meeting, the business idea is evaluated for viability, and the coach determines whether the entrepreneur has the necessary knowledge and whether he or she is willing to make the necessary effort to take the idea forward. Experienced consultants help entrepreneurs assess risk and opportunities. Entrepreneurs can expect answers to all of their questions related to their proposal, including how to found a company and what steps to take to move their business idea forward.

Phase two consists of creating a detailed business plan. The entrepreneur will discuss all relevant points with a specialist and create a professional business plan. This includes everything from the basic business idea to marketing and finances. The program has several specialists available from various areas, and entrepreneurs can choose who they want to work with. Both phases of the program are completely free of charge and are open to everyone, regardless of sector.

[Apply to] info@bplt.ch

[Links] Web: bplt.ch/kostenlose-beratung LinkedIn: company/bplt Facebook: bplt.ch

**Shaping the
future of hea**

www.dayone.swiss

#DayOneBasel
#InnovateInBasel

e collaboration with

on of Basel-Stadt

- Have a groundbreaking innovation.
  We're looking for never-before-seen digital
  solutions to pressing healthcare problems.

- Make sure it's tech-only.
  We don't support basic research, therapeutic-
  molecule-discovery projects, or drug-development
  projects (e.g., clinical trials of therapeutics).

- Show some entrepreneurial spirit.
  You don't have to be an established startup,
  but we want to see initiative from your side.

- Be experienced in the healthcare field.
  Your innovation should be based in
  healthcare expertise.

- Put patients first.
  We believe in a patient-centric approach
  to healthcare, and you should too.

[Name]	# DayOne
[Elevator Pitch]	*"We're an accelerator program that funds and supports innovative ventures in the fields of digital health and medical technology."*
[Sector]	**Digital health, medtech**

[Description]

High-tech nanosensors for glucose monitoring. Artificial intelligence for analyzing EEG charts. A baby translator that lets new parents know exactly why their child is crying. When it comes to applying technological innovation to the field of healthcare, there are countless possibilities – and the team behind DayOne is interested in them all.

Like BaseLaunch and i4Challenge, this initiative is run by Basel Area Business & Innovation with the goal of attracting top-tier entrepreneurs to the region. Its three verticals focus on digital health, medical technology and a handful of tracks that vary for each annual application round. For the 2020/21 round, for example, the focus was on value-based healthcare, patient-centric innovation and diabetes care. Applicants from across the spectrum are welcome: they can be startups, corporate intrapreneurs, or individual doctors or patients. The main requirement is that they have a promising innovation with proof of concept. Shortlisted ventures are asked to present their idea in front of a selection committee at the annual DayOne Conference in Basel. Out of over one hundred applicants per year, around thirty are shortlisted, and just six are selected for the accelerator.

Participants in the program must relocate to either Basel (for the digital health vertical) or the Canton of Jura (for the tech vertical). There, they undergo an intense six months of coaching, workshops, team building, networking and business model testing, usually while based at one of the Switzerland Innovation Park Basel Area sites. They also receive up to CHF 50,000 in direct funding and plenty of assistance in searching for larger grants and financing opportunities. The ultimate goal is to transform these healthcare innovations into standalone companies. Since the accelerator's inception in 2017, DayOne has helped launch more than twenty-three projects with a combined CHF 48 million valuation, most of which stayed in the Basel Area after the program was completed.

[Apply to]   dayone@baselarea.swiss

[Links]   Web: **dayone.swiss** LinkedIn: **company/dayone-healthcare-innovation** Twitter: **@BaselArea**

- **Be at the vanguard of Industry 4.0.**
  Whatever your product or idea, you've got to
  be able to connect it to the way we work now.

- **Have something to show us.**
  If you're a startup or SME, we want to see an MVP,
  prototype or finished product.

- **Have a customer-centric approach.**
  We want products and services that can be sold
  or offered to customers, no matter the field.

- **Come from Switzerland, Grand Est or
  Baden-Württemberg.**
  We're willing to expand our search into parts
  of France and Germany, but generally, this
  program is for locals only.

[Name] # i4Challenge

[Elevator Pitch] *"We're an acceleration program for SMEs, startups and innovators developing solutions, new approaches and next-generation products or services for Industry 4.0."*

[Sector] **Industry 4.0, IoT, robotics, AI**

[Description] AI, data analytics, virtual reality, IoT – these technologies are changing the way the working world operates. That's why Basel Area Business & Innovation launched the i4Challenge, an accelerator program specifically focused on companies and projects involved in this transformation, which is known as Industry 4.0. The program is divided into three tracks: one for SMEs that have already developed and sustained products or services; one for startups in the process of developing them; and one for new ideas from students, individuals and tech teams who have a promising innovation in the Industry 4.0 field but have not yet formed a company around it. Applications for all three tracks are evaluated on a yearly basis, with participants selected by a jury of industry leaders.

Participants with established products or services and those in the process of developing them receive mentoring, promotion and access to Basel Area Business & Innovation's network, as well as six months of coworking space in one of four Switzerland Innovation Park Basel Area sites. SMEs and startups are invited to exhibit at the BE 4.0 trade fair in Mulhouse, France, and are offered one year of free membership to the Mulhouse Industrial Society, as well as the possibility to appear as a keynote speaker at a Basel Area Business & Innovation event. In addition, participants can benefit from attractive education offers from connected universities. Participants in the new-ideas track go through a six-month acceleration program at Switzerland Innovation Park Basel Area Site Jura, in which they receive special support and tailored mentoring.

Since the program's inception in 2018, twenty-one companies and concepts from Switzerland, the French region of Grand Est and the German region of Baden-Württemberg have taken part. Notable alumni include BeWear, which uses AI to generate bespoke fashion patterns; drone-based inspection automation company Tinamu Labs; and No Touch Robotics, which has developed a sound-wave-based robotic gripper.

[Apply to] **i4challenge.com**

[Links] Web: **i4challenge.com** LinkedIn: **company/baselarea-business-innovation**
Twitter: **@BaselArea**

-   **Share our purpose.**
    Your startup or project should align with our
    values and goals. We want to collaborate towards
    a mutually beneficial outcome.

-   **Demonstrate proof of concept.**
    We want to know that your project has what
    it takes to succeed.

-   **Have a strong, confident and united team.**
    We believe we can only make long-lasting
    and sustainable changes as a collective.
    We want to see that your team can work
    together, and that it is united in its purpose.

-   **Have the focus and determination to see
    things through.**
    The startups that we partner with should show
    a determination and drive to succeed, and have
    the resilience and confidence to keep going.

-   **Be strategic.**
    We want to see that you and your team think
    beyond the day-to-day and that you look
    at the bigger picture.

[Name]
Innolab by Roche

[Elevator Pitch] *"We offer startups the opportunity to gain unparalleled access to one of the world's leading healthcare organizations and a chance to work closely with and learn from pioneers in the life sciences field in a collaborative and purpose-led manner."*

[Sector] **Life sciences, technology**

[Description] Innolab works with early-stage companies to give them the opportunity to work with and learn from one of the global leaders in the life sciences industry. Set up by the pioneering healthcare organization Roche in 2021, the startup engagement program was born out of a desire to create a collaborative space for startups and Roche to tackle global problems, and to build mutually beneficial partnerships. At its heart, Innolab provides startups with unparalleled access to unique expertise, support and guidance from Roche, and engagement with the external ecosystem, as well as the opportunity to partner on meaningful and world-changing projects.

Startups are invited to respond to open calls, which are based on topics that have been selected and identified by Roche as areas of interest for the business and its broader mission. Organizations are then shortlisted to attend a startup day, where they have the opportunity to pitch their ideas and solutions directly to leaders from Roche. During this day, there is also a series of workshops and talks, as well as an opportunity for companies that are further along in their startup journey to present to an expert panel. Successful startups then work with the Innolab team to develop their ideas further through pilot projects, and receive personalized and tailored mentoring and support from Roche. Innolabs runs its startup days twice annually and is always on the lookout for innovative and forward-thinking startups to partner with.

There also are two other avenues for startups to interact with Roche: the first is through the Venture Fund, which is the corporate investment division of the business that invests in life science companies, and the second is the Roche Partnering arm, through which the company collaborates with organizations that develop assets, products and services that are of interest to Roche.

[Apply to] roche.innolab@roche.com

[Links] Web: **roche.com** LinkedIn: **company/roche**

- **Translate your idea into a viable product or service.**
  The idea should make sense and be meaningful.

- **Demonstrate sustainability.**
  You should be able to demonstrate how the project can be achieved based on the available resources.

- **Have the right personality.**
  We're looking for young entrepreneurs who have self-discipline, are goal oriented, possess good resource-management skills and have good communication skills.

- **Be scalable.**
  You should be able to demonstrate potential scalability.

- **Be innovative.**
  We welcome innovative ideas and new ways of doing things.

[Name]
Startup Academy

[Elevator Pitch]
"We are a nonprofit organization that brings together people with business ideas and those with expertise and experience. We support, accompany and network with startups."

[Sector]
Sector-agnostic

[Description]
Startup Academy supports and connects startups from the founder's initial idea up to a maximum of twenty-four months. The program caters to all industries and sectors, and individuals from all backgrounds are welcome to apply. For CHF 80 per month, startup teams gain access to a wide range of benefits, including mentoring, training courses, workshops and networking opportunities, as well as the possibility of financial support and more.

Startup Academy relies on a network of 150 mentors and experts to help deliver the program, which consists of eight milestones. The process starts with participants identifying a business idea, then they move on to establishing a business model, testing it, identifying markets, building up a minimum viable product, and then entering the market. Startups typically stay in the program for up to two years. No startup is the same, so Startup Academy uses a tailor-made approach. It adapts its model and designs a roadmap for participants to follow, and each achieves the milestones on an individual basis. Participants in the program also have access to panels of experts, who look at the progress and provide feedback at every stage of the process. The program is very flexible and provides support in every area an entrepreneur might need help in, from legal advice to marketing, to name a few.

To date, over two hundred startups have been actively involved in Startup Academy's program. Its coworking site in Basel has fifty-five desks and several meeting and workshop rooms, as well as other facilities, where startups gather on a regular basis to share ideas and experiences.

[Apply to]
basel@startup-academy.ch

[Links]
Web: **startup-academy.ch** LinkedIn: **company/startup-academy-switzerland**
Facebook: **startupacademybasel** Twitter: **@SA_Schweiz** Instagram: **startupacademybasel**

- **Have a business idea.**
  It all starts with a business idea, so if you have one
  and want to know what to do next, get in touch.

- **Be located or willing to settle in the Canton
  of Basel-Landschaft.**
  Our offer is available in Baselland, so you need
  to be based in the area.

- **Don't hesitate in contacting us.**
  Sometimes we're not sure whether an idea is good
  or not, but we can help you find the right people
  and organizations to discuss this with you.

- **Be curious.**
  Take a look at what is going on in the Canton
  of Basel-Landschaft. You might just find what
  you're looking for.

[Name]
StartUp@Baselland

[Elevator Pitch]

"We're an entry point for anyone wanting to start a business in the Canton of Basel-Landschaft. We work as a directory of all the activities that the canton is sponsoring and supporting."

[Sector]

Sector-agnostic

[Description]

Launched in November 2019 at the University of Applied Sciences Northwestern Switzerland in Muttenz, StartUp@Baselland is an initiative that aims to promote the founding of startups and increase the innovative and economic power in the Canton of Basel-Landschaft. The initiative does so through joint activities with several partners, including a service that "is more or less like a directory," according to Robert Sum, deputy head of economic development at Kanton Basel-Landschaft.

A collaboration with the Baselland Economic Promotion, StartUp@Baselland works as a one-stop-shop where budding entrepreneurs and startups can find the support they require. Support for entrepreneurs and startups is provided by a number of business partners in the canton, namely Business Parc Reinach, Business Park Oberbaselbiet | Laufental | Thierstein, Startup Academy Liestal, and Basel Area Business & Innovation. These partners provide free consulting and coaching in various areas. Startups can also find office space within a professional environment, where they will be surrounded by other startups and be part of a thriving community. Another benefit is access to funding advice for anyone wanting to start a business.

StartUp@Baselland is not a specific program for which people and companies have to qualify. Instead, it caters to entrepreneurs and startups from all sectors, and anyone interested in entrepreneurship can benefit from the umbrella initiative. "You can be a hairdresser, an engineer, or the next Steve Jobs with a brilliant idea – what we can do is to provide you with contacts and point you in the right direction," Robert says. StartUp@Baselland also produces three or four roadshows each year. The partner organizations and selected startups have the chance to go on tour, showcase their work, and serve as inspiration for others. The aim of these events is to guide and motivate prospective entrepreneurs, and to provide them with the tools to start successful businesses.

[Apply to]
welcome@startup-baselland.ch

[Links]
Web: **startup-baselland.ch** LinkedIn: **company/startup-baselland** Facebook: **startupbaselland**

- **Have an innovative project.**
  We accept anything from new products and
  services to systems improvements, business
  ideas, management models and much more.
  If it's innovative, you're eligible.

- **Be no more than two years on the market.**
  Your product or service should have been on the
  market for less than two years but your company
  can be older. Exceptions can be made for products
  and services that have significant impact.

- **Have a convincing elevator pitch.**
  You'll need to present your project multiple times
  to a varied audience so you need to get their
  attention fast and leave them in no doubt as
  to why they should pick you.

- **Be creative, persistent, ambitious and ready
  to leave your comfort zone.**
  You'll need all these qualities to make it.

[Name]

Swiss Innovation Challenge

[Elevator Pitch]

"We are a free innovation support program that assists national and international innovators through an annual challenge competition. Our aim is to facilitate and accelerate the development, implementation and market entry of innovative products, systems, business ideas, services and more."

[Sector]

Sector-agnostic

[Description]

The Swiss Innovation Challenge is an initiative of FHNW University of Applied Sciences and Arts Northwestern Switzerland, Baselland Economic Chamber and the Basel-Landschaft cantonal bank. Founded in 2014, the challenge is open to everyone from startups and SMEs to NGOs, academic institutions and public administrations. The company structure and sector and the type and scale of the project are less important than its innovative nature. Basel's lively life sciences sector is well represented, but entrants also come from a range of other industries to ensure a truly diverse mix. Most participants are from Switzerland, but the program welcomes innovators from other countries. Notable former winners include AgroSustain, which focuses on ecological agrifood solutions, and Resistell, which tackles antibiotic resistance.

The challenge takes place over eight months and features three elimination rounds. At the end of each stage, participants pitch to a diverse jury drawn from finance, academia and the business and entrepreneurial world. Of the initial one hundred or more applicants, fifty will make it through to round two, and twenty-five will go on to compete in the final round for prize money totaling CHF 60,000. In addition to the main award, there are two special categories for life sciences and construction. All participants receive free coaching, mentoring, seminars on business topics and support and advice on planning, market entry and legal questions, as well as networking, marketing, PR and media attention. Detailed feedback is also provided after each round.

The Swiss Innovation Challenge has no registration fee nor any other financial obligations for participants, and is designed so participants can put their business first. The stages are long, with breaks in between, and participants can submit previously prepared materials, such as an existing business plan, rather than having to create everything from scratch.

[Apply to]

swissinnovationchallenge.ch

[Links]

Web: **swissinnovationchallenge.ch** LinkedIn: **company/swiss-innovation-challenge**
Twitter: **@sic_swiss** Instagram: **swissinnovationchallenge**

- **Be enrolled in an appropriate program.**
  The challenge is open to all students enrolled
  in entrepreneurship programs.

- **Teach at FHNW.**
  The competition isn't just for students – we also
  encourage our staff members to make their ideas
  a reality.

- **Have a viable project or idea.**
  We accept projects at both the idea and
  implementation stages, but our main criterion
  is feasibility.

- **Have the drive and determination to found
  your startup.**
  We're looking for aspiring founders with the will
  to see it through.

[Name]	# Swiss Startup Challenge

[Elevator Pitch]
"We are a public–private initiative that supports students and staff members at FHNW University of Applied Sciences and Arts Northwestern Switzerland to found or grow a startup. To this end, we provide prize money and resources through an annual challenge competition."

[Sector]
Sector-agnostic

[Description]
Founded in 2013, the Swiss Startup Challenge is open to all staff members at FHNW University of Applied Sciences and Arts Northwestern Switzerland as well as students enrolled in the university's entrepreneurship programs. Typically, these are undergraduate degree courses or summer and winter schools and programs run by the business school. At the end of each program, students pitch to their lecturers before the challenge management team selects ten to fifteen promising candidates for the competition. All selected teams must then submit a short self-produced video and a two-page summary of their business idea.

The challenge is judged by members of the Aargau Services Economic Promotion agency and UBS Switzerland bank (Aargau/Solothurn region). Prize money is put up by UBS, and the award ceremony takes place at the StartUpForum Aargau in October or November each year. The five finalists receive CHF 4,000 for first place; CHF 2,000 for second place; CHF 1,000 for third place; and CHF 500 each for fourth and fifth place. As well as competing for prize money, all participants benefit from coaching and gain valuable exposure.

The challenge is open to ventures in any sector but has a strong business focus. Many entrants come from the business school, but others are drawn from arts and design, life sciences, applied psychology, education and more. While the challenge is primarily for FHNW students, collaborations with other international universities mean overseas students enrolled in eligible FHNW programs may also take part. Some participants have founded startups and are looking to scale or expand to new markets, but most are pre-foundation. Notable former winners include marketing company Working Bicycle; nonprofit Backpack2school; Kumiko Kids, which makes fair, sustainable baby clothes; green retail finance company Tuyoh; and organic-pet-food provider Tschiri.

[Apply to]
stefan.philippi@fhnw.ch

[Links]
Web: **fhnw.ch/startupchallenge** Facebook: **SwissStartupChallenge**

VERLEIHUNG

SWISS STUDENT
SUSTAINABILITY
AWARDS
2019

- **Have a clear vision and be purpose-driven.**
  We want applicants to have a clear purpose
  and mission that will have a tangible impact on
  society or the environment and solve a social
  or environmental challenge.

- **Know your numbers.**
  You may not have a full business plan yet, but
  you need to know how you will fund your project.

- **Understand your market and get to know
  the competition.**
  We're looking for startups and project teams that
  are clear about their target audience and have an
  understanding of who the competition is in their
  field or area.

- **Acknowledge your strengths and skill gaps.**
  We're looking for teams that know their
  competencies and where their strengths lie but
  that also acknowledge where there may be gaps
  in knowledge or skills.

Swiss Sustainability Challenge

[Name]

[Elevator Pitch] *"We offer a unique sustainability program. Our aim is to support and mentor young entrepreneurs who want to develop their ideas and ventures into tangible projects and organizations that have a positive and sustainable impact on society and the environment."*

[Sector] Social entrepreneurship, sustainability

[Description] Established in 2010, the annual Swiss Sustainability Challenge competition is run by FHNW University of Applied Sciences and Arts Northwestern Switzerland in partnership with the insurance and pensions company Pax, Schweizerische Lebensversicherungs-Gesellschaft. The program supports and encourages young entrepreneurs and organizations to develop and realize their ambitions to create purpose-driven and impact-led companies and ventures. Through mentoring sessions, seminars and workshops, as well as a variety of tools, the program works as a launchpad for impact-focused entrepreneurs. Participants gain access to expert advice and a network of industry connections, as well as the chance to win a cash prize.

Open to startups, initiatives and associations, the entry criteria are simple: the project or organization must have a focus on sustainability and impact and at least one member of the team must be thirty years old or younger. In the first round, twenty teams are selected for an interview with a panel of three experts. Ten teams are then shortlisted and receive coaching sessions as well as access to tools to help them build and grow their idea prior to the final round. During the final, the ten groups have the opportunity to pitch their project to a panel, and three are chosen as winners of the Pax Sustainability Award. The overall winner is awarded CHF 10,000, while second place receives CHF 6,000 and third CHF 4,000. All three winners also receive a professional recording session to create a video presenting their project, as well as a sustainability assessment by FHNW.

A unique benefit of the program is that all applicants are automatically entitled to four hours of free coaching and also have access to a range of workshops and seminars led by a group of experts from across academia and industry.

[Apply to] sustainabilitychallenge.ch/en/anmeldung

[Links] Web: **sustainabilitychallenge.ch** LinkedIn: **company/swiss-sustainability-challenge**

spa

ces

[Name] # Business Parc Reinach

[Address]   Christoph Merian-Ring 11, 4153 Reinach

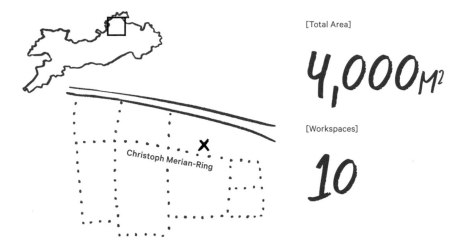

[Total Area]

4,000M²

[Workspaces]

10

[The Story]   Business Parc Reinach has been in operation since the early 2000s, but the origins of the coworking space came later, when IT specialist and musician Beat Gersbach was looking for a room for his company, Definition 12. He found a room big enough for his employees and piano, and thought it would be a good idea to share the space and even work on common projects with other creative entrepreneurs.

In May 2017, Business Parc Reinach started offering coworking space where startups and entrepreneurs alike can benefit from shared high-end facilities and member perks such as telephone and postal services. The space includes a total of 4,000 m² of office space, including 150 m² dedicated to ten coworking spaces. Members can choose between two options: Coworking Fix, which requires a rental period of at least six months, and Coworking Flex, which allows members to reserve a space for a certain period of time. Business Parc Reinach caters to a wide variety of business sectors, with members in IT, life sciences and technology, among others. It also offers free consulting for startups based in Basel-Landschaft – a team of experts is available to assist entrepreneurs through all stages of the startup lifecycle. Business Parc Reinach is developing a new building, which will provide space for fifty more companies.

[Links]   Web: businessparc.ch LinkedIn: company/business-parc-reinach Facebook: BusinessParc

Face of the Space:

Melchior Buchs has been the managing director of Business Parc Reinach since 2014. His background includes experience in PR, time as a municipal councillor and mayor in Reinach and numerous senior roles in various companies and organizations, including the umbrella association for Swiss medical technology. In 2010, he cofounded the communication agency Buchs & Sachsse at Business Parc Reinach.

[Name] # Impact Hub Basel

[Address] Münchensteinerstr. 274a, 4053 Basel

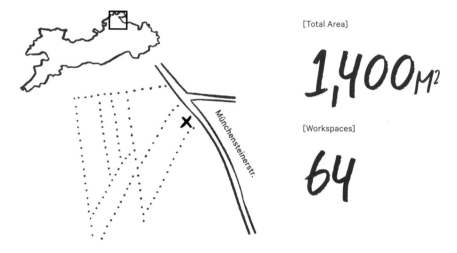

[Total Area]

1,400м²

[Workspaces]

64

[The Story] Founded in 2017, Impact Hub Basel started out as an association and community with a series of events focused on supporting social entrepreneurs, sustainable startups and purpose-driven innovators. In November 2019, in collaboration with Christoph Merian Stiftung, the organization opened a coworking and events space in Dreispitz. With sixty-four desks, a dedicated events venue, multiple meeting rooms, private phone booths, a community kitchen, outdoor terrace and a zero-waste cafe, the large and airy building offers a versatile, inspiring and welcoming space to work. Members can choose from a variety of flexible packages, including day passes, monthly hot-desk memberships and fixed-desk options. There are also special offers for students and associations.

The Impact Factory is the Hub's large event space, which can be hired on a half-day or daily basis and includes wifi, projectors and whiteboards, as well as video conferencing facilities. Community and connection are at the core of Impact Hub Basel's mission and it actively encourages and engages with members to create a collaborative, impact-driven ecosystem. Through a range of programs, projects and events, it offers support and assistance to individuals and organizations. From the Zero Waste Innovation Lab to an impact-focused incubator program, each project has a focus on driving change and making a positive impact on the world.

[Links] Web: basel.impacthub.net LinkedIn: company/impact-hub-basel Facebook: impacthubbasel Instagram: impacthub_basel

Face of the Space:
Tamara Waeber grew up on a farm
in the Fribourg region of Switzerland,
and her desire to travel took her
to Sierre, where she studied tourist
management. As Impact Hub Basel's
hospitality manager, Tamara enjoys
working in a team and supporting
others. She combines her interest in
providing a sustainable and inspiring
environment with a passion for hosting
and nurturing relationships with people.

Switzerland Innovation Park Basel Area

[Name]

[Address]   Gewerbestr. 24, 2nd Floor, 4123 Allschwil

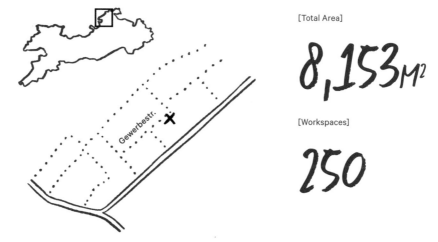

[Total Area]

8,153M²

[Workspaces]

250

[The Story]   Switzerland Innovation Park Basel Area was founded in 2016 as part of a network
of innovation parks created by the foundation Switzerland Innovation – an
initiative to promote research, development and collaboration between companies,
startups and universities in Switzerland. The park is spread across four sites
in the Basel Area. The focus of the main site, Allschwil, is biotech and medtech,
the Basel and Novartis Campus sites are home to digital health, and the Jura site
is focused on medtech, digital health, healthtech and industrial transformation.
A new Allschwil site will open as the main campus in 2022, where a new state-of-
the-art building designed by world-renowned architects Herzog & de Meuron will
offer 50,000 m² of office and lab space.

All sites offer a wide range of facilities, including office spaces, coworking areas,
private and shared labs, meeting rooms, lounges and cafeterias. Accelerator
programs also take place at each of the sites. "What differentiates us from other
coworking places is that each site has an accelerator, and we offer extensive
startup support services," says Karin Crisanto, head of innovation space
and infrastructure.

[Links]   Web: switzerland-innovation.com/baselarea
LinkedIn: company/switzerland-innovation-park-basel-area Twitter: @parkbaselarea

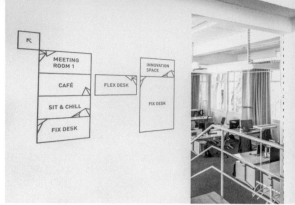

Face of the Space:

As head of innovation space and infrastructure, Karin Crisanto ensures that all services and operations run smoothly across all four sites, making sure that Switzerland Innovation Park Basel Area members have everything they need to successfully work, innovate and collaborate.

[Name] # Technologiepark Basel

[Address] Hochbergerstr. 60C, 4057 Basel

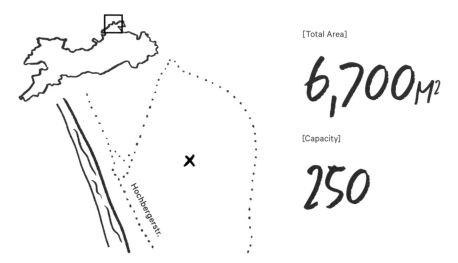

[Total Area]

6,700M²

[Capacity]

250

[The Story] Founded in 2011 by the Economic Development Section of Kanton Basel-Stadt, Technologiepark Basel provides office space and laboratories for startups on favorable terms. The canton saw an opportunity to develop a coworking space for technology and biotech startups that would otherwise face obstacles in setting up their laboratory or office. Located in Stücki Park, a unique innovation hub in northern Basel, Technologiepark has fully equipped, state-of-the-art laboratories with communal infrastructure and a range of dedicated offices for rent on an affordable and flexible basis.

The space includes breakout areas, kitchens, showers, a large auditorium and a variety of meeting rooms that can also be rented by nonmembers. Since its inception, Technologiepark has expanded three times and can now accommodate up to about 250 people. It attracts a mix of life sciences (particularly biotech and medtech) and IT companies, and fosters a collaborative and supportive environment. Occupants have the opportunity to attend Technologiepark's community-building program, which includes lunch and learn sessions and social gatherings, and are encouraged to become part of a friendly and open community. With the support of the Economic Development Section of Kanton Basel-Stadt and the innovation promotion agency Basel Area Business & Innovation, tenants have access to strong and relevant networks within the region.

[Links] Web: technologiepark.ch LinkedIn: company/technologiepark-basel

Face of the Space:
As CEO of Technologiepark Basel, Nina Ryser-Iten is passionate about supporting companies and individuals to develop their ideas and bring them to market. Having worked across a range of roles in innovation and economic development in the US and Switzerland and as cohead of the Economic Development Section of Kanton Basel-Stadt, Nina brings a wealth of experience to the role and a strong motivation to nurture and assist startups on their innovation and development journeys.

[Name] # The 5th Floor

[Address] Hofackerstr. 40B, 4132 Muttenz

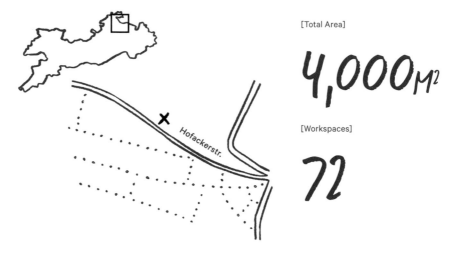

[Total Area]

4,000M²

[Workspaces]

72

[The Story] The 5th Floor coworking and innovation space is located on the top floor of the sitEX Powerhouse building next to FHNW University of Applied Sciences and Arts Northwestern Switzerland. It offers lockable cubicles, fixed and flexible desks, virtual offices and meeting, seminar, project and multimedia rooms. There's also a kitchen, communal area and rooftop terrace, and the CO.LAB community laboratory. The 5th Floor is home to a young, dynamic and diverse crowd of entrepreneurs and freelancers from various industries, including life sciences. The decor is appropriately professional but brightened up with splashes of color.

As well as daily and monthly coworking passes, sitEX offers a shareable family card with daycare and five hours of coworking a month included. Members can also access the Powerhouse gym, canteen, restaurant, post office, bike storage room and more. Proximity to Basel's pharma industry and FHNW, which is a source of young talent, is also an advantage. The 5th Floor hosts workshops and social events and, for selected companies, offers mentoring, coaching and access to funding opportunities via the inQbator incubator. For those wishing to expand overseas, there's a plug-and-play market-entry solution through international branches of The 5th Floor (currently, Orlando, Florida and Puerto Rico, with more on the way), which can connect members with partner service providers, including accountants, lawyers, IT and more.

[Links] Web: the5thfloor.ch LinkedIn: company/the5thfloor Facebook: @the5thfloor.ch
Instagram: the.5th.floor

Face of the Space:

sitEX Powerhouse property manager Claudia Armbruster brought her excellent people skills and years of experience in governmental property management to The 5th Floor in spring 2020. She's in charge of the day-to-day running of the entire 46,000 m^2 Powerhouse building and looks after its dynamic, diverse community to ensure everyone gets the most out of working in this all-inclusive "city within a city."

[Name] # The Manhattan

[Address] Route de Moutier 9, 2800 Delémont

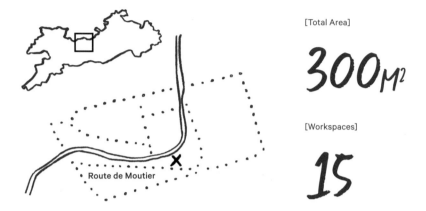

[Total Area]

300m²

[Workspaces]

15

Route de Moutier

[The Story] In the town of Delémont, situated in the hills of rural Jura about forty minutes outside of Basel, coworking was largely a foreign concept until Emilie Dobric came along. A young go-getter from the canton, she teamed up with the Jura government to establish The Manhattan, a cozy tech hive on the second floor of a high-ceilinged historical building close to the train station.

Opened mid-pandemic in October 2020, The Manhattan has approximately ten members who make use of its floating desks, while the conference rooms are populated by a rotating cast of startups from the Romandy region and beyond. It doesn't have the same networking opportunities as larger spaces in the center of Basel, but The Manhattan has everything you need to get remote work done in Jura's quaint cantonal capital: fast internet, printing capabilities, a soundproof phone booth and a chill-out room to provide peace and quiet. You can also mingle with the locals in the downstairs bar, appropriately named Brooklyn.

[Links] Web: themanhattan.ch LinkedIn: company/the-manhattan Facebook: themanhattan2800
Instagram: themanhattan2800

Face of the Space:

Emilie Dobric's path to managing The Manhattan began with a simple inconvenience: she was working remotely and needed access to a good printer. She now manages the space on a voluntary basis while continuing to work in marketing.

[Name] # Westhive Basel Rosental

[Address] Rosentalstr. 33, 4058 Basel

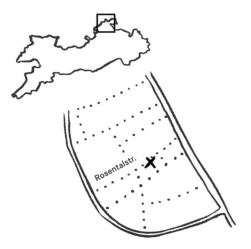

[Total Area]

2,500M²

[Workspaces]

220

[The Story] Westhive began in Zurich in April 2018, when the cofounders of a boutique digital- and growth-marketing consultancy were looking to set up a shared office space. After successfully launching in three Zurich locations, they set their sights on Basel and its lively life sciences and startup scene. Hearing that the well-connected central Rosental area was set for regeneration, they knew they'd found their new site. In April 2020, Westhive Basel Rosental opened in temporary premises, pending the launch of a larger permanent space in early 2022.

Westhive Basel Rosental offers fixed and flexible desks in team offices and a communal area. It also has formal and informal meeting rooms and lounges, a courtyard and event space. The decor is warm and welcoming with lots of natural wood, neutral colors, soft lighting and carpeting to keep noise to a minimum. Conscious that its tenants have busy schedules and limited funds, Westhive provides enterprise-level infrastructure for the startup pocket, and catering, leisure facilities, IT support and more are included in its transparent all-inclusive rates. A dedicated startup desk and a growth and digital marketing consultancy are also on hand to help Westhive Basel Rosental's diverse community of freelancers and companies of all sizes to grow and scale. As well as regular community events, tenants also gain access to the Westhive ecosystem of companies, service providers, investors and accelerators.

[Links] Web: westhive.com LinkedIn: company/westhive Facebook: westhive
Instagram: westhive_com Twitter: @westhive

Face of the Space:

Westhive cofounder and partner Claus Bornholt brings a wealth of experience in digital and growth marketing, as well as experience in managing coworking spaces. At Westhive Basel Rosental, he takes care of personnel, PR, marketing and communications, and sales and client relationships. Somehow, he and his cofounders find time to run their digital-marketing agency in between managing the coworking space and helping its members grow.

erts

Aligning solutions with corporate strategies can help startups collaborate for success

Sibylle Fischer / Director, Strategic Venturing at Baloise Group

Insurance and Banking

For startup founders looking to create innovative products and solutions or develop new ways of working, collaboration with a corporation can be a great starting point. Sibylle Fischer, director of strategic venturing at Baloise, suggests that startups in such a position align their solution with a company's corporate strategy.

A startup's ability to solve specific problems faster than a large corporation is a big advantage for the corporation, Sibylle explains, and by aligning its activities with a company's corporate strategy, a startup has an opportunity to benefit from the corporation's resources. She highlights the Baloise Simply Safe corporate strategy, which outlines the company's goals and initiatives, and guides how Baloise collaborates with startups. The Simply Safe strategy aims to make customers' lives easier and safer in the areas of core insurance and larger ecosystem of home and mobility. "Becoming a more agile, resistant and resilient organization underlies the whole strategy," she says.

Sibylle started her career in mergers and acquisitions at Deutsche Bahn, and joined Baloise in 2010. Since 2017, she's been part of the investment committee of Anthemis Baloise Strategic Ventures, the corporate venture capital arm of Baloise that manages a €100 million fund and invests in early-stage startups in the US, UK, Europe and Israel. Sibylle is responsible for corporate venture capital activities within Baloise and connects interesting startups with the business.

Using Baloise as an example, Sibylle explains that collaboration among startups and corporations can begin by matching a company's needs to startups in the market, or by having a startup approach the corporation with a clear problem and solution.

Most important tips for startups:

- **Do your research.** Find the right people to contact on LinkedIn or the Baloise Group homepage and make a short list of who you'd like to speak to.

- **Join an accelerator or incubator.** Many of these organizations have good connections to corporations in banking and insurance, and can make introductions on your behalf.

- **Work with other corporations.** Having proof that you've successfully worked with other corporations shows that you know how to make a successful partnership.

- **Be at the right place at the right time.** Sometimes we meet really interesting startups but strategically they're not part of our main focus at that moment. Read our latest media releases to find out what we're focusing on.

- **Build personal relationships.** Regularly catch up with your contacts, share what you're working on and let them know if you think there might be opportunities to collaborate.

Then, the corporation might run a proof of concept test that can turn into a long-term partnership or investment. In addition to this, Baloise partners with global accelerators and incubators to scout for innovative solutions, and Sibylle encourages founders to join these programs.

There are three areas Sibylle highlights as opportunities for startups to collaborate with corporations for financial innovation: improving the customer experience, diversification and sustainability. "Making the customer experience, in insurance and the larger ecosystem, seamless, safer and simpler is where I think founders have a lot of potential," she says. She also identifies mortgages and life insurance as areas where startups can have a big impact.

Sibylle explains that Baloise is always looking to collaborate with startups that can make it easier for customers to interact with the company. For example, in 2017, Baloise collaborated with startups KASKO and Picsure to create a single-item insurance product for watches using artificial intelligence. Clients can upload a photo of their watch and immediately receive an insurance quote. "From this, we developed single-item insurance where we have various partners that we can serve and deliver products with," says Sibylle.

Sustainability is a key element of Baloise's corporate strategy and an area where Sibylle believes startups can play a key role. One way the organization supports this is by investing in startups focused on climate protection. "They have a better risk return rate, deliver better financial results to us and have a positive impact on the environment and society," says Sibylle. For example, via Anthemis Baloise Strategic Ventures, Baloise invested in Stable, which provides insurance to farmers that compensates them for lost income due to price volatility.

When building relationships with internal stakeholders at corporations, Sibylle suggests founders stay in regular contact to provide company updates and present opportunities for collaboration based on the corporation's current priorities. "If the startup sees the right angle for collaboration, it's easier for us to find the right people within our group," says Sibylle.

About
Baloise Group is a provider of prevention, pension, assistance and insurance solutions. Baloise Open Innovation leads startup collaboration and investments for the group. Headquartered in Basel, Baloise Group's core markets are Switzerland, Germany, Luxembourg and Belgium.

[Contact]   Email: **sibylle.fischer@baloise.com**

[Links]   Web: **baloise.com** LinkedIn: **company/baloisegroup** Twitter: **@baloise_group**
Facebook: **BaloiseGroup** Instagram: **faktischversichert**

" *Making the customer experience, in insurance and the larger ecosystem, seamless, safer and simpler is where I think founders have a lot of potential.* "

Creating a clear strategy and vision for financial success

Michael Baumberger / Director, SME Clients at Basler Kantonalbank

Stefan Janczar / Senior SME Client Advisor at Basler Kantonalbank

[Sector] **Banking**

Startup founders can set themselves up for success by seeking out financial and accounting partners who are experts at helping businesses grow, and who are also aligned with the startup's vision and strategy. According to Michael Baumberger, director of SME clients, and Stefan Janczar, senior SME client advisor at Basler Kantonalbank (BKB), key factors in the success of an early-stage startup include working with the right people, identifying diverse sources of financing and good business planning. The right partner can help with all of these.

Michael leads the SME department at BKB, supporting startups and larger enterprises in the greater Basel area. Stefan brings over forty years of experience working directly with small businesses. They agree that it's important for founders to present themselves with confidence when approaching potential partners such as banks. "Potential partners look for entrepreneurs who have a clear vision and strategy for their business," says Michael, emphasizing the need for founders to be well prepared. They also suggest having a prototype or MVP that can be tested with customers to get valuable feedback, and Stefan adds that if the founding team can demonstrate experience in the market they plan to operate in, this can also help to build trust with new partners.

Having a clear vision and prototype can also help founders make meaningful connections within their local ecosystem network. Going into an event or meeting with a focused strategy and vision will help founders better explain their activities and help them to connect with relevant industry players. "Basel is a great place for startups and it's important to use the infrastructure that Basel has in place, including the network of mentors and financing options," says Michael.

Most important tips for startups:

- **Have an experienced, committed team.** The people behind the business should be ready to see the company through both the ups and downs.

- **Create a comprehensive business plan.** This should include the business case, market and model, and should be understandable for people who aren't familiar with your product, service or market.

- **Get funding from various sources.** This could be from your own savings, public grants, banks or venture capital. Banks, including BKB, can help you apply for loans with guarantees backed by the Swiss government.

- **Build a network.** Basel Area has a strong network of support for early-stage startups that is ready to help those just starting out. Reach out to local partners who can help accelerate your business.

Michael and Stefan acknowledge that securing initial funding can be
a huge challenge for early-stage startups, and they suggest that founders
look outside of family and friends for seed funding and apply to dedicated
support programs that can help them with initial research and applications.
One example is the KMUimpuls program offered by BKB. Created in 2006,
the program provides assistance to both startups and scaling enterprises looking
for financing, including access to public funds. An example of public funding
is Bürgschaftsgenossenschaft, a guarantee cooperative provided by the Swiss
government for loans to early-stage startups. This means that a portion
of the loan is guaranteed to be paid back by the government if a startup does
not succeed, significantly reducing the risk of the loan to providers. As part
of KMUimpuls, startups can also begin making repayments on loans at a later
date, giving them more time to become stable.

A clear business plan and model is another vital part of attracting partners and
achieving success, and something else that BKB can assist with. "The business
plan should be understandable for someone who doesn't know what you do,
or the market your product or service is targeting," says Stefan. BKB has partnered
with Startup Academy to help founders create effective business plans and
clear models. BKB recommends that startups who approach them for funding
participate in Startup Academy, and its team provides mentoring to entrepreneurs
who participate in the program.

One successful example is Golex, the startup behind Sens2Go. This biofeedback
system helps patients successfully recover after surgery on their lower limbs.
Golex was supported by Basel Area Business & Innovation, Startup Academy
and BKB. In 2019, Golex approached BKB for support. The startup was already
part of the Startup Academy, had the support of the Swiss Health System for
its product and was expanding to Germany. In 2020, BKB supported them with
a public financing program, and in 2021, it granted Golex another financing round
for the growth of the company.

About

Founded in 1899, Basler Kantonalbank provides banking and financial services
to private and corporate customers in the greater Basel region.

[Contact]   Email: **kmu@bkb.ch** Telephone: **+41 (0) 61 266 38 86**

[Links]   Web: **bkb.ch** LinkedIn: **company/baslerkantonalbank** Twitter: **@BaslerKB**
Instagram: **baslerkantonalbank**

"Potential partners look for entrepreneurs who have a clear vision and strategy for their business."

Build user love of product through iteration and experimentation

Ilya Shumilin / Cofounder at Wild Ma-Gässli

Dina Andriatis / Cofounder at Wild Ma-Gässli

[Sector]   **Design consulting**

While mentoring startups at Mass Challenge, Ilya Shumilin, cofounder of Wild Ma-Gässli, noticed a pattern among the companies he was working with. "One thing that's the same for early-stage startups is they don't pay enough attention to user experience in their product," he says. He worked with these startups to help them understand that good user experience (UX) design is significantly more than just screenshots and using design software. "It involves a lot of research. You need to be responsive to feedback, and you must be ready to iterate," he says, adding that in his experience, companies need two to three iterations to make meaningful progress. For Ilya and Wild Ma-Gässli cofounder Dina Andriatis, this is the only way to successfully build products, and was the inspiration for them founding their product-design company, which is named after a small street in Basel.

Dina and Ilya have worked together on digital projects since 2014, and founded Wild Ma-Gässli in 2021. Dina has a master's in architectural lighting design, has worked on lighting-design projects across Europe, and has been working in graphic and UX design since 2012. Ilya has master's degrees in physics and computer science, and previously worked at fintech lab Keen Innovation.

"UX is how the user feels about the app," Dina explains. Ilya says that creating good UX requires a deep understanding of who a company's customers and users are before beginning any development work. The customer isn't usually the founder and their family or friends, who, in his experience, tend to be the people the founders have built the initial product for. Additionally, Dina and Ilya say that UX should be a core component of any product that a company builds, not something that's thrown in at the last minute. "The user experience isn't up to one person to write," says Dina, adding that it's a process involving iterations and conversations with customers and developers.

Most important tips for startups:

- **Iterate as much as possible.** It takes courage to constantly throw away what doesn't work, but it's the most important thing to build into your mindset to succeed.

- **Stay open to feedback.** It can be difficult, but taking feedback is an essential skill that will help you continue to grow as a leader.

- **Experiment often.** This is more than just changing the colors on some buttons. True innovation happens when you try the most daring of ideas.

- **Don't take anything personally.** Whether a design doesn't work out, or you hear critical feedback, it's important to remember that none of that is about you.

Iteration and experimentation are at the heart of creating a great UX according to Dina and Ilya. "It's important that startups understand they may have to change before they launch their product," says Ilya, explaining that such companies will uncover important variables that can change their product as part of this process.

To create a great UX, founders should start with researching their competitors. Next, they need to accept that they don't know everything when it comes to their product and mentally prepare for customer feedback. Then, they should seek out feedback on the prototype from people outside of their friend and family groups. They can do this by hiring a company to recruit and run user interviews where prospective users get to try out the prototype and explain where it works well and where it doesn't for them. Finally, founders should take this feedback, iterate on the prototype and present the new one to users. According to Ilya, this iterative process should continue until the feedback is 90 percent positive from users before starting development.

For example, at Keen Innovation, Ilya worked on the UX of taxjungle.ch, a tool that helps expats navigate the complex world of taxation in Switzerland. Starting from scratch, the project went through seven or eight iterations based on usability tests and customer feedback before the product was launched.

At the early stages of prototyping, Dina and Ilya believe failure will be – and should be – high. "The real failure will be if you waste two years to build something that no one wants," says Ilya. "Pivoting is not a failure – it's improving, it's iterating." To psychologically prepare for feedback during the iteration and experimentation process, Ilya and Dina suggest that founders understand that no feedback is personal. They say that practicing meditation can help to find peace of mind and inner calm. When founders shift their mindset to embrace failure, truly understand who their users are and regularly ask them for feedback on the UX, they'll be able to iterate faster and eventually create a UX that their users will love.

About

Wild Ma-Gässli is a product design consultancy based in Basel. It creates engaging user experiences for corporations and startups, financial and tech companies. Through a structured research, prototyping and iteration process, it helps companies design products that customers love.

[Contact]   Email: **gruezi@wildma.ch**

[Links]   Web: **wildma.ch** LinkedIn: **company/wildma**

" *Pivoting is not
a failure – it's
improving, it's iterating.* "

Novartis Campus:
Join a network of
life-sciences innovators

Matthias Leuenberger / Country President Switzerland at Novartis

We're opening up Novartis Campus, bolstering a new network where biotechnology, life sciences, digital healthcare and research institutions of all sizes can work side by side to enhance the standard of medical care for patients around the world. This is a network where connections are made, knowledge is shared and ideas are pushed forward.

The opening up of the Novartis Campus is closely associated with our cultural transformation – a transformation to a more open, communicative and collaborative culture. Our campus will establish itself even more strongly as a campus of knowledge – a place of encounters and interaction. Proximity and conversations inspire new thinking, new approaches and ultimately more innovative products. For example, we want to tap into the potential of big data and digital solutions in development, research and the provision of drugs in a way that enables faster diagnosis and treatment of patients worldwide. As partnerships are increasingly important in this environment, with the opening we would like to invite every associate to engage in new forms of exchange. Together, we are reimagining medicine.

The Novartis Campus in Basel is the site of our global headquarters. It is a space for dialogue, collaboration and scientific progress. It is characterized by its vibrant working environment and unique atmosphere, encompassing parks, restaurants, cafés, events spaces and sports facilities.

Since 2020, we have opened up the campus to companies working in the fields of life sciences and digital solutions in healthcare. In a second phase planned for autumn 2022, Novartis Campus will be made accessible to the general public during our working hours. This second step will allow the public to experience Novartis Campus and further strengthen the exchange between Novartis, external companies and the general public.

Novartis is investing heavily in the ongoing development of our campus in Basel. The Novartis Pavillon, a building that is a place of encounters and knowledge, is our symbol for the opening towards the public, hosting an exhibition on the wonders of medicine and featuring space for events and lectures for a public audience. Two large lab buildings are currently being completely redesigned, and a number of different spaces in lab buildings are being modernized and modified. The research teams will be able to establish new ways of working and new colocation concepts in the new buildings. Individual lab buildings on the periphery of the campus will be made available for external rental or as a location for external real estate development.

Basel – a place for life sciences

Novartis Campus is set in Basel, a city that's been the beating heart of the European life sciences community for decades. With seven hundred companies, institutes and universities, the Basel region is already one of the most important centers of life sciences expertise in the world today. Located on the borders of Germany and France, the Swiss city is a thriving hub of scientific development, world-leading education and rich culture.

We expect that the opening of our Novartis Campus and the settlement of startups and other companies will further strengthen the region's economy. Physical proximity promotes exchange and thus innovation.

New ways of working

The conventional understanding of office work will be less location-based in the future and will take place in a wider variety of spatial concepts. New technology and forms of collaboration enable greater mobility. With Choice with Responsibility (CwR), Novartis invites its associates to decide independently, in coordination with other members of their teams and in line with their tasks and legal frameworks, when, where and how they can work best to carry out their responsibilities. According to our surveys, associates want to have more flexibility to choose between working in the office on the campus and working from home or at another location. This means that many associates will no longer spend every day, or the whole day, at the company premises. We expect that the new ways of working and CwR will reduce the space requirements of Novartis teams in the office buildings, but that the variety in terms of usage options will increase.

A campus that inspires collaboration

Novartis Campus is designed to unleash the power of people. It's a place where big ideas happen and progress is made – a natural space for experts to come together and forge new paths. So how are we fostering collaboration on campus?

- Novartis Campus lets you embed yourself in a network with like-minded people. A sense of scientific openness combines with communal spaces to encourage conversations and encounters that can open new possibilities and spark new working relationships.

- The life sciences network at Novartis Campus will be home to a diverse group of people and organizations, all with their own unique skill sets and unique ideas. From biotech to digital health, bold startup founders to seasoned academic researchers, it's a rich melting pot of knowledge, experience and ideas.

- Working alongside your fellow experts offers opportunities to collaborate and interact through accelerators, incubators, training and pitch sessions. They'll be a chance for you and your peers to harness the knowledge, resources and experience of each other, and of Novartis.

Novartis Biome: Collaboration for patients

Too many patients are waiting too long to get the medicines and treatment they need. We can change that – but we can't do it alone. By working together with patients, healthcare providers, healthcare systems and the best of the tech ecosystem, we can better understand, anticipate and deliver on their needs.

The Novartis Biome represents a network of innovation hubs around the world that unites the best of science and technology to find, build and scale better healthcare solutions and patient experiences and bring them to patients in a way that is as innovative as our science. The Novartis Biome is the bridge between the tech community and Novartis. Our target is to develop solutions to improve the lives of our patients.

The most important aspect of any successful partnership and collaboration is dialogue. It's incredibly powerful how a shared sense of purpose can fuel amazing innovation, especially when there is an open and transparent conversation. This trust is what enables us to shape and grow an amazing community with our ecosystem and healthcare-system partners. We can't and don't want to go on this journey on our own, so come join us – imagine what we can build together.

[Contact]   Email: communications.switzerland@novartis.com

[Links]   Web: novartis.com | campus.novartis.com LinkedIn: company/novartis
Facebook: novartis Instagram: novartis Twitter: @novartis

foun

ders

Danuta Cichocka

CEO, Cofounder / Resistell

Polish-born Danuta Cichocka's career path was decided as a child, when tonsil surgery left her with an antibiotic-resistant infection that took years to treat. Later, she gained a PhD in microbiology and worked in research before serving as a research program officer at the European Institution. After returning to academia, she earned an executive MBA and a certificate in management of biotech, medtech and pharma ventures at École Polytechnique Fédérale de Lausanne (EPFL). She then approached EPFL's Laboratory of Physics of Living Matter to commercialize breakthrough antibiotic-susceptibility testing technology, and founded Resistell in 2018.

Why the switch from academia to business?
My husband is an entrepreneur, so I was always exposed to the startup ecosystem and he encouraged me. I was also very interested in the applied aspect. Research is very interesting to a certain point, but to really have an impact, a startup is much better than academia.

I knew a lot about startups and I knew that a new venture in life science or healthcare is a very complex project, much more than startups in other fields. It's heavily regulated and involves a lot of knowledge from very different fields. I knew which problem I wanted to solve, and I wanted to prepare because I knew how difficult it is to launch a new venture. I knew my academic background was good enough but I didn't feel ready to launch a business. The MBA gave me this toolbox. I knew where to start, how to search for technology, validate it and do those first steps towards the startup.

What challenges did you face in the early days?
One of the biggest challenges was that the topic of antibiotic resistance was not really popular in Switzerland. When I started, in 2017, in the startup world there was a lot of attention given to cancer and not many investors interested in startups in infectious diseases. Neurodegenerative diseases were also a hot topic. In the last few decades, most of the big pharmaceutical companies withdrew from R&D in new antibiotics because it was not profitable anymore. When I started, anything related to antibiotics and antibiotic resistance was considered highly unprofitable and not interesting for investment. That was a very big challenge.

After my MBA, I knew about startup accelerators like Venture Kick and MassChallenge. I participated in multiple accelerators and even the coaches who focus on life science and healthcare didn't consider it very promising from a business point of view, for return on investment.

What changed?
I took part in a brand new startup accelerator called Swissbiolabs. The technology is based on atomic force microscopy, which has a lot of history in the Basel region. There were people who knew this technology and they found the application for antibiotic resistance extremely interesting, and I won first prize. This really accelerated development because I got connected with the local ecosystem. I received a lot of support from the Basel region, a coach, lots of advisors. There was a small financial prize, but they made a huge poster next to the train station in Olten with the name of the company, and this had a much bigger impact than the money. This and this publicity I received made a huge change.

How did you fund the company initially?
Equity. I didn't have any grants. EPFL did, so the research was well funded, but for the startup it took two years until I closed the first financing round. During these two years, I won many prizes, but usually a very small amount, not something that allows business development.

I invested a lot of personal resources because in the first years I had to finance all the travel and conferences. The fact that my husband had an IT company helped. His company created the first websites, PR, visual identity, etc. I think it's very important to have some personal resources in the beginning because closing the first financing round takes a lot of time, and it's very difficult to close in reasonable conditions if you have nothing – you need to have leverage for negotiation. So I decided to spend some time and invest from the private pocket.

When I closed the financing round, I had already won many competitions, I had a solid business plan and the option agreement for the technology license. I did a lot of work on the patent (because it wasn't granted yet) with the technology transfer officer at EPFL to accelerate it.

How many funding rounds have you closed to date?
Three. A seed round at the end of 2018, then a Series A round at the end of 2019, and now an extension of the Series A round. We did get a lot of grants, but much later. People think you can initially fund the company by grants and then open the financing round, but here it was completely the other way around.

"*Basel is a world-famous hub for the pharmaceutical industry. Especially for companies at a slightly later stage like ours, it's important to be close to the relevant industry.*"

We first closed the seed round, and this allowed us to raise a lot of non-dilutive funding. Most grants for companies require a cash contribution, which founders, people from academia, are not aware of. Before this extension of the round, it was fifty percent from the investors and fifty percent from non-dilutive sources.

What are the most rewarding or challenging aspects of your role?
The most challenging is financing. Finding the resources is the most important role of the CEO. Once you have funding, you can hire people for everything, but not before. So, attracting attention to the project, visibility from competitions, networking and fundraising. This is one of the key roles, and it's very difficult because the majority of founders come from academia and they have completely different profiles – what they enjoy most is scientific research. It is also something I'm very much involved in and really enjoy. A year ago, I was still partly leading the microbiology research and preparation for clinical validation, but the more mature the company is, the less I'm involved in this part.

What are you most proud of?
My team and the infrastructure we have. We have almost twenty operational prototypes built. In three years, we managed to build a team of twenty people, including microbiologists and engineers. We were able to prove the repeatability of this technology and bring it to the clinical stage. In May 2021, we started the first clinical study. Without the team, none of it would be possible. I'm also very proud that in September 2020, we opened brand-new laboratories in Muttenz in the sitEX Powerhouse.

What's next, and when do you go to market?
A pilot clinical study for the first bacteria and antibiotic combination. Next year, we will run the main study for various combinations of antibiotics and bacteria. Once we have that, we can officially launch the device onto the diagnostic market. In the meantime, we are planning to launch the device for research and start commercialization. In 2022, we will be able to certify it and launch it for diagnostics. We are also starting to look for industrial collaborations for further development of the technology for other applications.

Is there more interest now?
Now it has completely changed. After COVID-19, infectious diseases are at the center of attention. We had a complete shift from lack of interest in antibiotics to really big industries actively searching for technologies for antibiotic susceptibility testing because it's a very big issue. Many COVID-19 patients treated in intensive care units receive broad-spectrum antibiotics as prevention of hospital-acquired infections, especially patients who are artificially ventilated. It's really sad that we needed this pandemic to bring attention to this issue because it's a very old topic.

Knowing what you know now, what would you do differently? Any advice for others?

I would close the round sooner. It's really crucial for a startup to have the first funding quickly because the world is changing – there's always new competition coming up. In the startup ecosystem, people always think about direct competition in their field, but not about competition for funding. Very often it's other topics that are the center of attention, and this is very important. So if I could share any advice with founders, I would say: if there is momentum, if suddenly people are interested in the topic, just grab the opportunity and raise funds, because it's a very short window of opportunity.

What makes the Basel Area a good location?

Close proximity to industry. Basel is a hub for the pharmaceutical industry. Especially for companies at a slightly later stage like ours, it's important to be close to the relevant industry. We are also next to the Fachhochschule building, which is fantastic because we have access to young people. We hire a lot of people for internships, bachelor's and master's theses, and many stay with us. Basel has good access to the workforce – it's in the cross-border region so there is a lot of diversity here. Because of the pharmaceutical industry, there are a lot of foreigners. Diversity is extremely important for a startup.

The location is fantastic for microbiology skills, and there is a lot of support for young companies, which is very valuable. These support services exist in other cantons, especially Zurich and Lausanne, where we have ETH [Swiss Federal Institute of Technology] and EPFL, but there is also a lot of competition for support. In Basel, there is much less competition and fewer startups, so support is much more accessible and things go faster. I think it's a very good opportunity to locate the company in the young ecosystems, the new startup hubs, the places which will grow but are not at the limit yet.

[About]   Resistell is a medical-device company whose innovative technology cuts time-to-results for antibiotic-susceptibility testing from days to hours. This means doctors can prescribe the right antibiotic sooner and avoid creating resistance by administering ineffective treatments before accurate information is available to guide decisions.

[Links]   Web: resistell.com LinkedIn: company/resistell
Facebook: Resistell-614545495406609 Twitter: @Resistell_

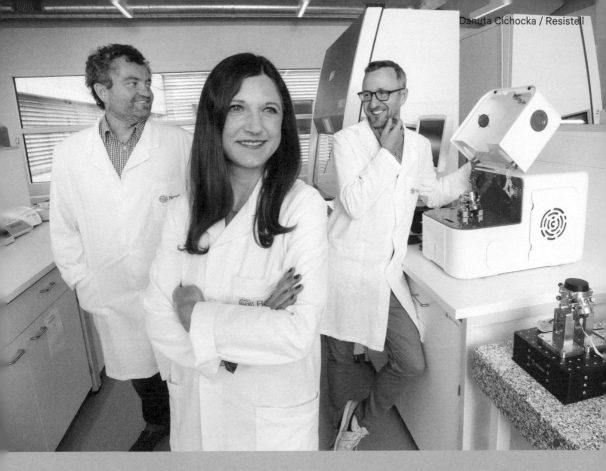

What are your top work essentials?
iPhone and laptop.

At what age did you found your company?
Thirty-seven.

What's your most-used app?
WhatsApp.

**What's the most valuable
piece of advice you've been given?**
Never give up. Be persistent.

What's your greatest skill?
Analytical thinking and being able to connect
the dots, connecting multiple complex subjects.

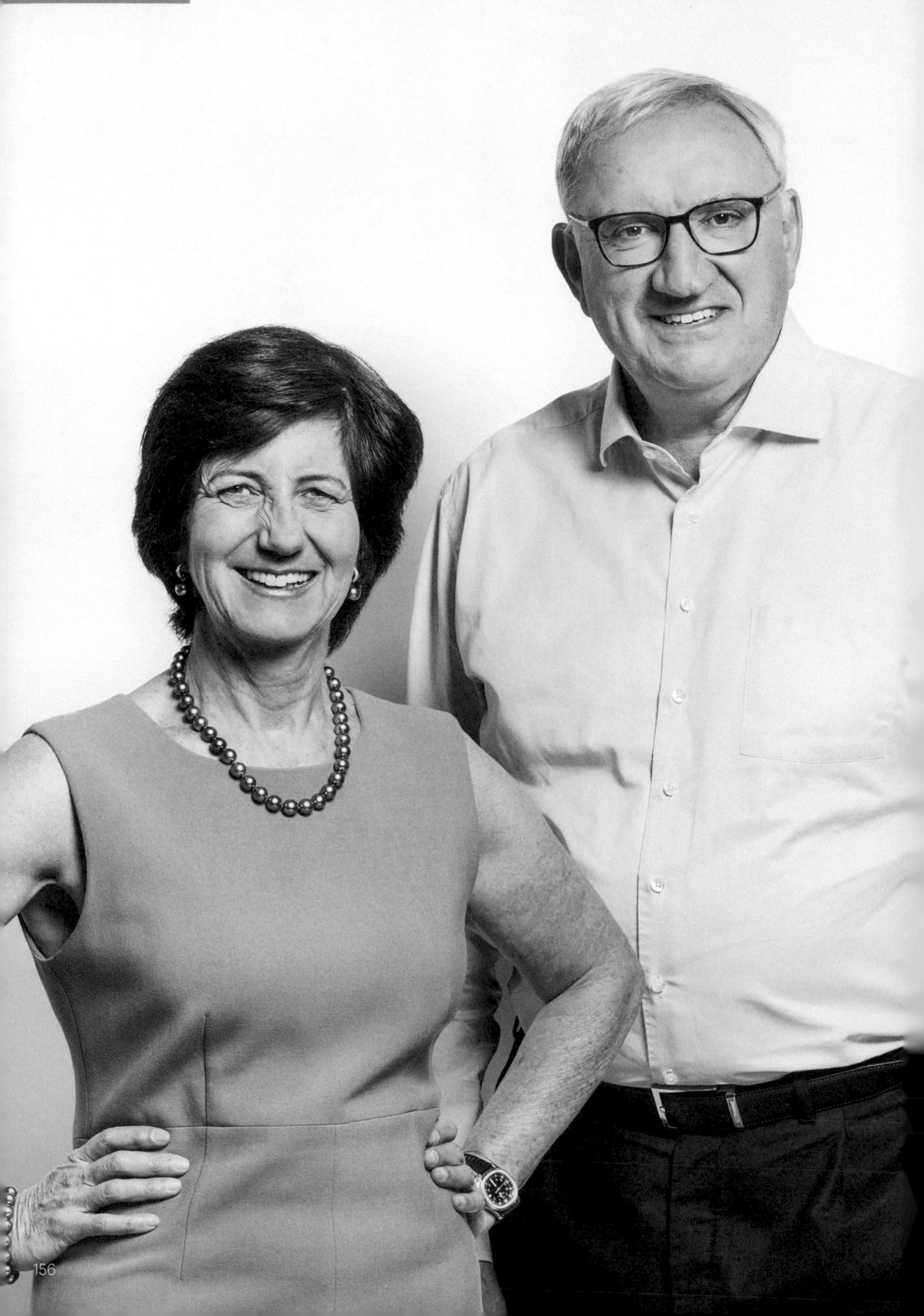

Jean-Paul Clozel & Martine Clozel

CEO / Idorsia

Executive Vice President and CSO / Idorsia

Jean-Paul and Martine Clozel met while studying cardiovascular medicine and pediatrics, respectively, in their native France in the 1970s. Further training and research in pharmacology and physiology at prestigious institutions, including McGill University and the University of California, San Francisco, followed before they returned to Europe to lead drug-discovery teams at F. Hoffmann-La Roche in Switzerland. When one of Martine's discoveries had applications for Jean-Paul's cardiovascular medicine department, they began to collaborate. In 1997, they cofounded Actelion with Walter Fischli and Thomas Widmann.

What spurred you to leave Roche and cofound Actelion?
Martine: We were already thinking about creating a new company to be able to drive decisions about R&D when we discovered several new compounds, new mechanisms of action. My main topic was endothelin, and that was really Actelion's first success, but we had several projects in mind at the time, which allowed us to think about starting a lab; not just a company, but really starting research.

Jean-Paul: The four of us wanted to do research. We had witnessed the creation of Genentech and Apple. We were in San Francisco – you were always discussing things with startups. There was never a startup in Switzerland, and I thought this was a different way to do research. We also had the important discovery of endothelin, but it was mainly a decision to do something different from the big companies. Twenty-five years ago, power was what was driving these companies, the Pfizers of the world, GSK and so on. Commercial power was their main attribute – you had to be big. But suddenly scientific innovation started to take over and we saw that by being innovative, you could compete with big companies.

Martine: There were some big startups, big biotechs – not startups anymore, Genentech, Amgen, maybe the beginning of Gilead – but they were based on antibodies. They were putting their discoveries into motion themselves, doing clinical development and marketing. We wanted to do that but with small molecules.

Why did you set up in Basel?

Martine: One of the founders was Swiss and we were French. All of us had been more than ten years in Roche in Basel and we knew chemistry was very good in Switzerland.

Jean-Paul: If you want to be in fashion, you should be in Paris or Milan. If you want to be in finance, you'd better be in London or New York. If you want to be in pharma, Basel is maybe the city with the biggest concentration of pharma discovery and business in the world.

What else does the city offer for businesses like yours?

Martine: Many aspects, but I will say one word: diversity. It's very important to have diverse cultures, diverse origins, and it was important for us to have the possibility to grow with diversity.

Jean-Paul: Basel has always been at the intersection of several countries, so we have a lot of German researchers and collaborators, French collaborators. It's an intellectual city where you can find not only scientists but artists. Thinking, drug discovery and innovation are really part of the culture.

What were your greatest achievements with Actelion?

Martine: Our first oral drug compound for pulmonary arterial hypertension. Bringing the first oral drug for a disease that had no treatment except a very cumbersome one. And then bringing other drugs to patients – that's the biggest satisfaction you can have as a doctor who starts a pharma or biotech company based on research.

Jean-Paul: The beginning and the end. In the beginning, we had the dream to create a real company with affiliates in Japan, the US and Europe with research. I thought it was never possible. It's like creating a car company: Tesla made it, but this is the exception. It was impossible to think you could compete against Ford, against Renault. We were competing against Roche, Novartis, Merck, GSK. I think that's really something I was proud of, because we succeeded. At the end, we were bought by Johnson & Johnson, but we could create Idorsia. No one lost their job, no project was stopped. Johnson & Johnson got the drugs they wanted, which is good for the patient. In such an acquisition, this is the only time that's happened. It's unique in the pharma industry, that the commercial part and the drugs went to Johnson & Johnson but they let us continue our research projects.

"*Don't do it for money – you will fail.*"

What convinced you to sell?

Jean-Paul: We didn't want to sell but finally we had no choice because it was for the investors. But for the patient, the solution that we found was reasonable.

Martine: It was the best outcome we could find to have Johnson & Johnson satisfied, but it was of course necessary for all the employees to be happy about the result in the end, because nobody was going to lose their job. A huge satisfaction was that all the people in research and early development could continue with the new company, Idorsia.

What are the challenges of creating a spin-off like this?

Jean-Paul: It was not easy. It would have been much easier [for Johnson & Johnson] to buy everything and not care about the projects. To separate patents, buildings, contracts... we had forty thousand contracts to deal with; you cannot imagine how difficult that was. If they put a price on the total thing, there would have been no negotiations, only the price. Here it was all aspects: which product goes where, which patent goes where.

Martine: It's only possible if you have a portfolio. We had this portfolio of research behind our approved compounds, which made it possible to create a new company, but this time with six hundred people, not just four, and ten compounds in development.

Jean-Paul: You also have things like Switzerland's flexibility in the laws that allowed it. There are some countries where there would have been taxes on the creation of Idorsia that would have made it impossible. And it's not just us; all the top management and the employees also decided to join Idorsia. If people had taken their money and gone to lie on the beach, there would have been no Idorsia. You need years to create such management. Also the social aspect: In the US, if you are sick, you need to have good insurance, so money is much more important. In Switzerland, scientists can remain long term. They do not always try to optimize their income. You do not have to decide only because of money.

How is the experience with Idorsia different to setting up Actelion all those years ago? What learnings do you bring to it?

Jean-Paul: Most of our failures [with Actelion] were due to being a young company – when you start from zero, often you don't have many choices. You have one product, you have money for six months, you don't have a choice of decisions. You have to do it and take some risk, which you won't when you are Idorsia with a rich and robust pipeline. If one fails, it's not a drama. In Actelion, it was a fight every single day. It was anxiety for me as a CEO because I had no choice. This is not the case in Idorsia. It's a startup that is three or four years old with research that is twenty years old.

What funding have you raised for Idorsia?

Jean-Paul: We started with CHF 1 billion in cash. Part of that was a convertible note from Johnson & Johnson with a nominal value of CHF 580 million. The rest was cash out of the Actelion war chest. Since then, we've done two accelerated book builds for around CHF 300 million each. We did another book build in October 2020 for around CHF 500 million plus. When we did the first transaction, it was accompanied with a CHF 200 million raise as a convertible bond, which is tradable. Added up, it's roughly CHF 1.4 billion in four instruments over three years.

Any advice for other founders?

Martine: Don't start alone. We had the team from the beginning, which was very important. Also, you need to be very pragmatic and find solutions, because a lot of questions come on the financial side, on the realization-of-milestones side. You need to think big, see the long term and find a way to survive short term. See what you could become.

Jean-Paul: Don't do it for money – you will fail. Just do it because you love science, you love innovation and you want to bring something to the patient – that's the right motivation. Also, it's great to start a company but you'd better know what you're doing. Too many people start in pharma or biotechs without knowing what they're doing. Our business is very regulated, with many components where experience really helps.

[About]   Idorsia is a pharmaceutical company that discovers, develops and commercializes innovative medicines based on small molecules for a range of conditions, including rare and orphan diseases. Idorsia was created as a spin-off when Actelion was acquired by Johnson & Johnson in 2017.

[Links]   Web: idorsia.com LinkedIn: company/Idorsia Facebook: Idorsia Twitter: @Idorsia

What are your top work essentials?
Jean-Paul: Good collaborators.
Martine: People who want to do research for patients.

At what age did you found your company?
We were both forty-two when we founded Actelion,
and sixty-two when we founded Idorsia.

What's your most-used app?
Martine: WhatsApp.
Jean-Paul: Everything included in Office 365.

**What's the most valuable
piece of advice you've been given?**
Jean-Paul: That a company's most valuable asset isn't
on the balance sheet but it's the most difficult thing to
create: the culture.
Martine: That people need to have trust, to know they
are supported by management when they take risks.

What's your greatest skill?
Jean-Paul: Being positive.
Martine: The desire to always be learning.

Marc Gitzinger

CEO, Cofounder / BioVersys

Originally from Luxembourg, Marc Gitzinger studied biology in Germany and
Australia before taking a role as an associate intern at management consultancy
McKinsey & Company. There, he gained valuable experience in business
planning and market research and entry in the medical-device sector. Returning
to academia, he obtained a PhD in biology at the Swiss Federal Institute
of Technology (ETH) in Zurich before moving to Basel with his department.
In 2008, he founded BioVersys as a spin-off from his research on synthetic
biology. Today, he is a thought leader in the field of antimicrobial research and
development, and vice president and board member of important life-science-
industry alliances.

Why the stint at McKinsey & Company?
I wanted to see what else I could do with my biology studies other than just
classical lab research, and I wanted to learn a bit more about how business works.
It was really interesting and satisfactory, but I realized I had unfinished business
in the research arena, and that brought me back to my PhD thesis.

When did you realize your PhD could lead to a viable business opportunity?
For a while, I was hoping that the work we do in the lab could eventually lead to
a drug that really saves patients' lives. That was a driving force in my thoughts.
Then one thing led to another: we had some ideas and technologies we could
actually use, and we understood that antimicrobial resistance is a very big unmet
medical need. This led me to start thinking that it would be great to test whether
we could actually start a company. But I didn't know how. That led to another great
Swiss thing called Venturelab. I followed the first of their courses and realized,
"Hey, it's actually possible." You get a bit of a toolbox, everything is a bit naïve,
but it takes away that huge barrier of not knowing how to get started.

You won several awards, including two Venture Kicks and the Swiss Technology Award. How did that help?

I took the opportunity to do a lot of these courses and prizes, and Switzerland has a lot of these business-plan competitions. That was extremely useful because we won quite a few. The first nearly half million in cash that we got was from the different business-plan competitions. We even incorporated the company maybe a bit too early because one of the prizes required that. So we did it and had this company formed before we were really ready to start operations, but we didn't regret it because it helped to get the first cash in and we could leverage that. Then came further innovation research money from Innosuisse. That's how we managed to get our first employee while we were still at the university. And then, half a year later, we moved out of the protective environment of the university and started the company for real. We moved into our own labs, found investors and so forth.

Was it hard going it alone?

At the time, there weren't too many hurdles. The Technology Park in Basel had just opened and we were among the first tenants. That was obviously brilliant because you had small and expandable lab spaces to rent with no long-term leases. Everything was flexible and really made for startups and spin-offs, which was really helpful. The infrastructure and all the publicity we got via the business-plan competitions helped us tremendously in raising our first seed-financing round really fast. The university was very helpful. We didn't have any hurdles in our way. Quite the opposite – we had plenty of opportunities. Switzerland is a great place to start companies, and Basel – particularly for life sciences or biotech – is really a fantastic place.

Why do you think Basel is a great place to start a company?

It starts with the government in Basel – the canton understands life sciences much better than many others. The timelines when they ask for tax or rent support and so forth, all of this works really nicely in Basel. They have great infrastructure and they're continuing to build more in and around Basel; spaces with labs and offices. Generally speaking, the government, especially here in Basel, realizes how biotech works and what we need. Everything is easy because they understand the business perfectly. During the COVID-19 pandemic, Basel was the only canton that offered high-tech and biotech companies a financial aid loan system that actually worked and was used by companies.

"*Entrepreneurship
is such a great thing
for society, for a country,
for individuals.*"

Another reason why Basel is really great is the access to talent. You cannot underestimate that. Thanks to the two big pharma companies, but also the many large and smaller companies in this field, there's so much talent. From technicians right up to very senior employees and advisors. So when you grow the business and look for very experienced senior people, even if you have to bring them in from the US or other European countries, you have an advantage being in Basel. Because, yes, you are a small company, which is riskier. People moving their whole family and life to Basel for this little company, it's a bit of a hurdle. But everyone realizes, "Okay, if this doesn't work, in Basel there are plenty of jobs. So I can move the family and take that risk more easily."

What milestones have you achieved so far?
One of the things I'm really proud of is that the first program, based on which we started the company, entered clinical trials last year. It was just incredible, that realization that I worked on this during my PhD on the bench and now it's administered to humans. That was something that I was honestly really proud of and a great moment for all of us in the company.

Now we cross our fingers and hope that we continue and eventually see that we actually save patients' lives, which was the original drive and idea. Antimicrobial resistance is a topic close to my heart because it's very important. As a company, we take this seriously. We develop programs for hospital-acquired infections in the developed world, as well as for diseases like tuberculosis, focusing on global health. COVID-19 has shown the impact infectious diseases can have on our daily lives. Unfortunately, despite the high unmet medical needs, there are still lots of problems on the economic side for antibiotics, as they are underpriced. I hope politicians understand that preparedness for pandemics and the value of antibiotics is not simply putting them on the shelf and having them not work. Antibiotics are the underlying medicine that we need for most of our medical advances today. Without working antibiotics, we cannot do the simplest surgeries anymore, or administer many of the modern cancer treatments.

What factors have been key to your success?
Funding is the obvious one that you need as a lifeblood. One of the biggest challenges in creating a company, especially in biotech, has to be the financing. You need specialized investors and you need deep pockets, especially when you start clinical trials. It's a true challenge to raise this kind of money and get used to thinking in these kinds of figures. Of course, your technology or your research also needs to be successful – that is a prerequisite.

A key success factor was hiring the right people, and realizing that we need to hire very experienced people. So we have created a team, a great mix, with a lot of very experienced people in leadership roles. Because the pharmaceutical industry is so regulated, and also so broad in the different types of expertise you need, you just can't put a price on experience.

Would you do anything differently if you were starting over?
Occasionally, I ask myself if we left the protective environment of the university a bit too early, because you can potentially do the early-stage research a bit longer in that environment. But being forced to stand on our own feet and be all alone and compete for funding, recognition, and move the project along as fast as possible helped us tremendously. If we hadn't had that kind of pressure, would we be as successful? I'm not sure.

You're also a Venturelab trainer and startup coach. What advice do you give to aspiring founders?
I am extremely grateful to Venturelab. I have benefited from them and other coaches and senior advisors whom I was lucky to meet along my path. Without this support, I think it would have been much more difficult. So besides the fact that it's a lot of fun to pass on some of your knowledge and experience, it's even a duty. Entrepreneurship is such a great thing for society, for a country, for individuals. I just feel really passionate about it. Continuing to bring younger people or people who are just starting their endeavor into entrepreneurship is a lot of fun, and I'm very happy to do it. I talk a lot about building teams and hiring the right people, working with your board of directors, working with advisors. The team is what makes the difference in the end. My point to founders is: really consciously take time to think about how you want to lead a team. Consider what the culture in the company should be and what kind of diversity of expertise, etc. you need.

How would you describe the culture in BioVersys?
We have a very mission- and vision-driven culture. We really know where we want to get to. Then, we allow for mistakes. We have an open culture around mistakes – we don't blame, and we talk about this very openly.

[About]   BioVersys performs research and development of new drugs in the field of antimicrobial resistance. Its aim is to address urgent unmet medical needs, including superbugs such as tuberculosis, ESCAPE pathogens and hospital-acquired infections from antibiotic-resistant bacteria.

[Links]   Web: bioversys.com LinkedIn: company/bioversys-ag Twitter: @Bioversys

What are your top work essentials?
Motivation and optimism. And then the tech stuff like
the iPad, phone and computer, of course.

At what age did you found your company?
Twenty-eight.

What's your most-used app?
Microsoft Teams and Zoom.

**What's the most valuable
piece of advice you've been given?**
Listen to advice but always own your own decisions.

What's your greatest skill?
Asking the right questions.

Roger Meier

CEO, Founder / Clarena

Originally from eastern Switzerland, Roger Meier showed early entrepreneurial promise by selling his paintings to neighbors while still in kindergarten. At fifteen, he was apprenticed to a Swiss bank advising high-net-worth individuals. After stints as a securities trader in Geneva and an investment banker on Wall Street, he earned a degree in economics and business administration before joining PricewaterhouseCoopers, where he advised multinationals on risk management. After helping a friend find a job, he realized the commercial potential of talent brokerage and founded Clarena. Today, he is an active member of the Swiss life sciences community, has cofounded twelve companies – including Acthera, Aurealis, Cellestia, Elthera, Kinarus, Nemis, T3 Pharma and Versameb – and has helped thousands of people navigate professional change or turn their ideas into startups.

How did you get into the startup world?
About fifteen years ago, someone said, "Roger, I don't really fancy a new job; I have an idea." I found the person great and the idea sounded convincing, but I couldn't tell whether it was feasible or not. I'm just a humble economist. So I reached out to my network to check whether the idea was valid, and whether we could implement it, which validated and de-risked the project. By then, I had built up a wide, trusted network to ask for advice, and I also provided that network with exclusive access to a potentially groundbreaking idea and the opportunity to join the startup team. So, I started to build a cloud of knowledge and goodwill around an idea that lifted it towards entrepreneurial execution, in a situation where there's no money, no resources at all. Startup founders usually lack everything: knowledge, money, a plan. How do you get it? By trust. I could provide that for innovators. From then on, things evolved and the word spread.

You're still providing those services. How does it work?
Trusted network partners usually bring me ideas. By reaching out to the network, ideas become projects, which become startups. For instance, now I'm looking for somebody to lead a stem cell company we're hoping to found. In parallel to team building, communication is key. Scientists and technicians communicate differently to financial people.

They're not keen on giving you a reason to invest because they would rather do the experiments first. There are different ways to tell your hypothesis, and I'm good at that – translating projects and ideas into stories that ordinary people can digest, at all levels: elevator pitches, factsheets, etc. The next step is reaching out to trusted contacts with high-definition power who can endorse people and ideas. Before we go and ask for money, we build trust.

After fifteen years, I have a very broad network of people with the additional knowledge startups need. They need a lot of skills, but not full time. You need people to defend your valuation, check patentability, etc. Postdocs might not have access to the right people, but if I ask my IP lawyer, for example, to have a look at something, he'll do it because we have a longstanding relationship. So, because of trust, I can motivate people to invest some sweat into startup projects in the beginning, which usually results in a great collaboration later. That's how we get a solid start before we look for investors.

How else do you help companies find investment?
Many years ago, I started to establish a funding system that was a bit new. The normal way companies fundraise is to go from one pitching event to the next. The usual response for early-stage companies is, "Sounds interesting, come back later when you've got more data. And you are too expensive." We do it differently. We do our homework first, properly. Then we start to talk to potential investors well before the financing round. If there is sufficient interest, we go ahead, testing the valuations first. Normally, we start with a subscription period, like securities, and say, "Look, this is when we start and you've got a month or two to make up your mind. The valuation is this much. Are you in or not?" This may seem a self-confident way of raising startup funds but it works because we team up with investors first. It's worked dozens of times. All the companies and projects I've been involved with, at foundation or growth, have probably raised above a billion Swiss francs in total.

Did you intend to get into life sciences or was that an accident of being in Basel?
I've been listening to peoples' life stories for years, and nobody really had a plan for what they want to become one day. Usually, people just made the best of a situation. My situation was talking to very interesting people with great ideas and bringing them together to implement a great project in a place with a 150-year history of trial and error. With many bright minds here, it is obvious the priority would be life sciences because trial and error are in Basel's genes. Not many areas have continuously evolved through different stages of industrialization and are still big. In the UK, the textile industry disappeared. Here, it evolved into dyestuffs, dyestuffs evolved into chemistry, chemistry involved into drugs and medicine. Then, the biologists came in, and that's why Basel is by far the richest city in Switzerland.

"If you have an idea you believe in, try to show it to the best possible people. And if they like it, never give up."

Being from a financial background, is it challenging to understand the high-level science biotechs deal in?

Of course, I had to learn a lot. I like learning, and I think curiosity is one of my main drivers. As a kid, I wanted to become everything. I couldn't make up my mind. I will never be a biochemist, but I think I'm good at asking stupid questions. After fifteen years, you learn by experience and thousands of hours of interaction with some of the brightest minds in our industry. Every human is different, every brain is different, and even the brightest scientists can be wrong in a highly qualified way. Many of them have very insular capacities and skills, but what they lack is connecting the dots and looking outside their comfort zone. That's where I and others come in. After so many years and thanks to strong networks, I have learned a lot, often the hard way, and I know many knowledgeable people. So if I don't understand anything, I can assess whether I must understand, whether I want to understand or if I've got people in my company who can understand. Consciously dealing with the unknown is a core element of any innovative industry.

What challenges have you faced?

One challenge is to make people outside of our community aware of what we do. In the Basel area, we are happy to have a lot of support and understanding. But wider Swiss society lacks understanding of the huge potential of our industry. There are many clichés, like why don't we have so many startups in Switzerland? The cliché is that the Swiss are not such risk-takers as others. But we are a cosmopolitan society and it's just not true.

Sometimes I feel Switzerland doesn't see where the free market isn't working. The life sciences industry accounts for over fifty percent of Swiss exports, with trade margins other industries can only dream of, so it's by far the most important. But if I look at what the country does for the translation of ideas into companies, it's very modest. In contrast, in the US, billions are invested into the incubation of companies and to pay practitioners, not only academics. This enables the foundation of many very valuable companies. In Switzerland, practitioners who join startup teams are not paid during the incubation phase, which is very limiting. The average incubation time of any startup I'm involved in is between one and three years, so the incubation phase is quite precariously financed. I think Switzerland could do something about that.

Another challenge is the absence of institutional and domestic funding. Our pension funds are sitting on a trillion of assets, but nothing is invested in early-stage life sciences, which doesn't make sense. If these holes in the ecosystem were filled, this area could excel and create much more value for society.

You've achieved a lot. What are you most proud of?
I'm happy we succeeded in establishing a COVID-19 loan facility that is considered to be one of the best industry programs in the world. Otherwise, I'm tremendously happy to contribute to incredibly interesting and good people. I'm standing on the shoulders of giants, and sometimes this dwarf has to whisper into their ears, and they listen and we go on. Also, throughout the years, I was able to help people change their lives. And every patient who responds is motivation in itself. I say I helped many people end up in good jobs, but I do believe I have the best job.

Is there anything you would do differently now?
Probably look a bit more deeply at overcoming my own bias. You tend to fall in love with ideas and people and so might overlook things. I would probably listen more to my gut and say, "This gentleman or lady has not really walked the talk. Shall I question their integrity?" Founding a startup is like falling in love. In the beginning, there's the honeymoon and we are so motivated. The challenges come over time.

You're also a coach and mentor for Innosuisse and the University of Basel. What's your top tip for founders?
If you have an idea you believe in, try to show it to the best possible people. And if they like it, never give up. Because if you convince really great people, they will bring in other great people and your thing will fly.

[About] Clarena was founded by serial entrepreneur and investor Roger Meier as a talent brokerage before expanding to provide networking, incubation and ideas validation for entrepreneurs. By leveraging Roger's extensive local and international network and knowledge of life sciences, finance and business, Clarena helps startups access talent, partners, funding and more.

[Links]   Web: **clarena.net** LinkedIn: **in/roger-meier-52032a**

What are your top work essentials?
Coffee, Zoom, iPhone and a notebook.

At what age did you found your company?
Thirty-one.

What's your most-used app?
Email and Outlook on my phone, and messaging apps.

**What's the most valuable
piece of advice you've been given?**
"It's good, but you can do better." This was from
my mother when I was in primary school.

What's your greatest skill?
I'm incredibly curious and I can reimagine
and connect the dots that bring people together.

ools

- **Be open minded.**
  If you want to succeed, you need soft interpersonal skills as much as hard professional know-how.

- **Want to solve problems.**
  Our students are problem solvers. If you have a deep desire to find solutions, you will fit in at FHNW.

- **Adapt to change.**
  We can guarantee that our courses will change. Adapting to change and being ready for the future are key components of any successful student.

- **Emphasize your willingness to learn.**
  Studying at the FHNW requires motivation and drive. We want our students to be eager to explore, experiment and learn.

- **Have a passion for innovation.**
  You need to have a passion to conduct innovative projects. Passion is a main requirement.

[Name]

FHNW University of Applied Sciences and Arts Northwestern Switzerland

[Elevator Pitch]

"We are one of Switzerland's leading universities of applied sciences and arts. Our broad range of programs, hands-on concept, innovative, application-oriented research and global network make us a diverse educational institution and a sought-after partner for industry."

[Enrollment]

Total enrollment: 13,161 (2020)

[Description]

FHNW was founded in 2006 by the four cantons of Aargau, Basel-Landschaft, Basel-Stadt and Solothurn, and has campuses in each location. Initially, five universities joined together: Aargau University of Applied Sciences, the University of Applied Sciences beider Basel, the Solothurn University of Applied Sciences, the School of Education and Social Work and the Solothurn School of Education. The Academy of Music and the Schola Cantorum Basiliensis later joined.

Renowned for its applied sciences and interdisciplinary collaboration among its schools, FHNW offers twenty-nine bachelor's programs and eighteen master's programs, as well as a range of continuing-education courses. Programs include life sciences, engineering, business, education and psychology, among others. A bachelor's in international business management allows students to study in Germany, France and Switzerland with instruction in three languages.

Students undertake real projects from industry, gaining first-hand experience and the opportunity to broaden their professional networks. FHNW also offers a range of projects, platforms and activities for its students. The three Swiss Challenges programs ask students to develop innovative business ideas while supported by experts. The Swiss Startup Challenge, Swiss Innovation Challenge and Swiss Sustainability Challenge are free to enter, and the programs provide comprehensive support, including workshops, networking events and mentoring.

[Apply to]

fhnw.ch/en/degree-programmes

[Links]

Web: **fhnw.ch** LinkedIn: **school/fachhochschule-nordwestschweiz-fhnw**
Twitter: **@FHNW** Facebook: **fhnw.ch**

- Speak French.
  There's a reason we don't have an English-language website – all of our courses are taught in French.

- Have experience.
  All our students must possess a Swiss school-leaving certificate or its equivalent qualification, and must have obtained at least one year of professional experience in the relevant field or completed a foundation year.

- Be passionate.
  We're looking for students who can demonstrate a strong interest in and aptitude for their chosen field – would-be engineers shouldn't be afraid of physics, math or chemistry, for example.

- Want to work.
  If you're looking for a purely theoretical education, the Haute École Arc isn't for you – we want students here to have a hands-on experience.

[Name]
Haute École Arc

[Elevator Pitch] *"We are a university of applied sciences with specialist programs in engineering, management, health and conservation-restoration, and a focus on hands-on, real-world experience."*

[Enrollment] **Students per year: 2,600**

[Description] Founded in 2005, the Haute École Arc is a network of four campuses spread across Jura, Neuchâtel and French-speaking parts of Bern. As a part of the larger University of Applied Sciences Western Switzerland, it accepts students who are following the Swiss vocational education program, meaning that most candidates have completed a three-year apprenticeship in their chosen field and received a *matura* (high-school) certificate. The majority of students come from the surrounding cantons, but a small number of foreign students also enroll each year, not counting those who come on exchange programs from partner universities around the world. All courses are taught in French.

The school offers bachelor's programs in nursing, as well as in the conservation-restoration of museum artifacts and, most interestingly for those in the startup realm, engineering and management degrees. Management students can earn a bachelor of science in business economics, management information technology, and – a specialty unique to French-speaking Switzerland – economic law. Post-graduate options include an Executive Master of Business Administration in management and leadership, and certificates in a range of areas including experiential marketing to supply-chain management. Engineering students can obtain a bachelor's degree in microengineering, industrial design, industrial engineering and management and IT, or a master's in industrial technologies and information and communication technologies.

No matter the area of study, know-how and experience are the foundation stones of HE-Arc's offerings. The school has a mission of nurturing talented young people on a daily basis by enhancing their scientific, technical, social and interpersonal skills. It has a strong focus on practical real-world applications, and most university staff members are involved in research. Aside from the conservation-restoration program, which is limited to a small number of students, the school accepts all applicants with the necessary qualifications. The cost is approximately CHF 500 per semester.

[Apply to] **he-arc.ch**

[Links] Web: **he-arc.ch** LinkedIn: **company/hauteecolearc** Facebook: **HauteEcoleArc** Instagram: **hauteecolearc** Twitter: **@Haute_Ecole_Arc**

- **Think big, think global.**
  Show us that you are thinking beyond local
  and regional borders.

- **Stay hungry, stay curious.**
  Always be open to learning, and be open to new
  perspectives.

- **Focus on impact.**
  Don't focus solely on financial goals. Think
  differently. Think sustainably. Do something good
  for the world.

- **It's a marathon, not a sprint.**
  You have to be committed for a long time to see
  the rewards.

[Name]
University of Basel

[Elevator Pitch] *"We are Switzerland's oldest university and are highly regarded for our research across science, medicine and technologies. We have an exhaustive list of higher education offerings, and encourage entrepreneurship among our students."*

[Enrollment] **Total enrollment: 13,139 (2020)**

[Description] The University of Basel is home to seven faculties covering a wide spectrum of academic disciplines, and offers a vast range of higher education courses. The institution also encourages entrepreneurship among its students. In recent years, the university reports an increase in interest in entrepreneurial thinking and activity that is no longer limited to natural and medical sciences, but also includes fields such as psychology and cultural management.

The university offers both bachelor's and master's degrees in business and economics, as well as a master's in business and technology and an interdisciplinary sustainable-development course. Further, the Innovation Office offers a number of entrepreneurial educational programs that include events and courses created in collaboration with Innosuisse, the Swiss innovation agency. These include the Innosuisse Start-up Training program, a twelve-week course delivered twice a year, in which students learn the basics of entrepreneurship. In addition, the university hosts several regular Innosuisse events focused on topics such as raising awareness and motivation, among others.

The University of Basel's Innovation Office also supports up to four projects a year with the Propelling Grant of CHF 50,000. The grant is intended to support early-stage projects based on scientific discoveries and with a clear startup trajectory, and is offered alongside an entrepreneurial skills-building program. This program also includes workshops delivered by industry experts in relevant topics. In addition, participating startups are connected with supporters and coaches from the entrepreneurship ecosystem. In 2019, the University of Basel launched FEMtrepreneurs, an initiative that fosters female entrepreneurship and provides women with the tools to get their businesses off the ground. It aims to empower and support female entrepreneurs, to give them visibility and to connect them with the ecosystem. Since 2021, the federal Office of Gender Equality has supported the initiative in hosting a series of workshops and events on entrepreneurship and beyond.

[Apply to] **innovation@unibas.ch**

[Links] Web: **unibas.ch/en/Innovation** LinkedIn: **company/unibas-innovation** Facebook: **unibasel** Instagram: **unibasel** Twitter: **@UniBasel**

- **Have a thirst for knowledge and self-development.**
  We are looking for participants who are eager to
  learn and who have a desire to continually improve
  and develop both professionally and personally.

- **Be open minded and committed to the program.**
  Participants on our programs need to have
  an open mind and be willing to work with people
  from all backgrounds. We are committed to creating
  an inclusive learning environment for all.

- **Demonstrate interest in entrepreneurship.**
  At Unternehmer Campus, we want our program
  attendees to demonstrate a solid interest
  in entrepreneurship and a drive to succeed.

- **Actively engage with the community.**
  We are looking for people who take part in
  the programs to become actively involved in the
  alumni community, to share their own knowledge
  and expertise, and engage in the network.

[Name]
Unternehmer Campus

[Elevator Pitch]
"Our unique programs support entrepreneurs, managers and company successors to develop and further their careers. From the seed of an idea to growing and leading a business, participants benefit from individualized mentoring and guidance from a wealth of industry experts."

[Enrollment]
Participants per year: 62

[Description]
In 2015, the *Gewerbeverband* (trade association) for Basel-Stadt saw an opportunity to address a gap in talent and training. People in management positions were moving into retirement and young professionals were leaving because of lack of opportunities. To assist businesses and entrepreneurs, the Gewerbeverband founded Unternehmer Campus. Through its fully subsidized programs, the organization offers participants the opportunity to grow and develop, both professionally and personally.

With support from industry experts and a one-of-a-kind career-development offerings, Unternehmer Campus runs two support programs each year: YoungPreneur and YoungLeader. YoungPreneur is aimed at young people undertaking apprenticeships and on-the-job training, and the YoungLeader program is offered to anyone over the age of eighteen who has already completed an education. Participants in the YoungLeader program come from all backgrounds: they can be at the start of their professional development journey and simply have an idea for starting a business, or they could already have spent years in their profession.

In the YoungLeader program, participants have access to support and assistance over an eight-month period. The program encompasses a broad range of topics, from how to write a business plan to more holistic themes such as ethics and mindfulness. All of the modules and workshops are led by industry experts, who assist the participants on their journey. Everyone who undertakes the YoungLeader program is also given the opportunity for one-on-one mentoring and coaching sessions, as well as the option to join an alumni community. All programs are free, and there are twenty-two places offered in each program per year.

[Apply to]
camptum.ch

[Links]
Web: **campus-unternehmertum.ch** LinkedIn: **groups/13579726**
Facebook: **Unternehmercampusbasel** Instagram: **unternehmer_campus**

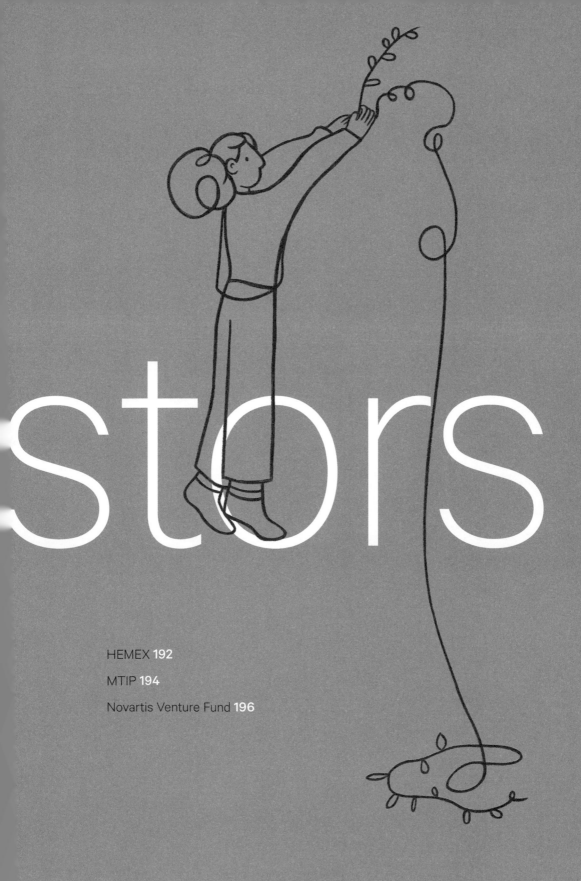

stors

- **Stand out from the crowd.**
  We're looking for original solutions that have never
  made it to market before. If you've patented yours,
  terrific. If not, we can help you with that.

- **Have a reasonable business plan.**
  No pie-in-the-sky projections – we just want
  to know your goals for the next few years.

- **Meet a need.**
  The more surveys you've done to prove there's
  demand for your product, the better.

- **Have a great presentation.**
  We get a lot of pitches, so you'll need to make sure
  yours really pops.

[Name] # HEMEX

[Elevator Pitch] *"From investment to clinical trial management, acceleration to marketing, we provide healthcare startups with everything they need to get their product from bench to market."*

[Sector] **Healthcare**

[Description] Founded by a trio of veterans from the pharmaceutical and medical-device sectors in 2015, HEMEX is far more than an investment firm. In addition to providing pre-seed and seed funding to promising life sciences startups, its team offers a range of other services: marketing, grant writing, conversion rate optimization, help navigating regulatory bureaucracy and more. HEMEX startup scout Mohamed Hussien compares the company to a supermarket in its variety of services.

Since March 2020, the easiest way to gain access to the full range of HEMEX benefits has been to apply to InQbator, an acceleration program founded through a partnership among HEMEX, the Basel bank BLKB, and the Singapore-based private-equity firm Launchpad. Early-stage startups enter at the Ignite phase and receive six months of coaching, mentoring and other assistance at a coworking space in Muttenz. More advanced startups can skip straight to the intensive Boost phase, during which they receive support with fundraising and gaining market access, as well as the chance to participate in exchange programs in Singapore and the US. Startups at any stage are able to take advantage of HEMEX's expertise and network, as well as receive discounts on its services. Graduates of the acceleration program may also receive direct funding.

HEMEX supports startups in any area of healthcare, whether it's pharma, biotech or even veterinary medicine, and from anywhere in the world, although in some cases relocation might be required. HEMEX is committed to changing the future of healthcare by guiding the most promising European startups and empowering them to drive change in both human and animal healthcare. In 2020 and 2021, many of the participants worked on new detection methods for COVID-19. Hussein says that applicants have a high chance of acceptance if they can prove their innovation.

[Apply to] hemex.ch/services

[Links] Web: **hemex.ch** LinkedIn: **company/hemex-ag** Twitter: **@HEMEXtwitt**

- Clearly be in our target scope.
  You need to be a healthtech, digital health or digitally connected medical-device company.

- Be located in Europe.
  We are not limited to any one country, but the company must be based in Europe.

- Have an exciting solution.
  We look for solutions that are unique in the healthcare market. Decentralization of care and corrective or preventive medicine are things we care about.

- Present a scalable and sustainable solution.
  The scalability of the solution is important, and your company must have a scalable business model.

- Be at the right stage as a company.
  You should be able to demonstrate initial market traction with recurring revenues.

- Have a team with the right mindset.
  We see ourselves as partners of the management team, so it's important to have a robust team that is receptive to our guidance and willing to develop.

[Name] # MTIP

[Elevator Pitch]
"MTIP is a healthtech growth capital investor with a track record of scaling up successful and sustainable businesses. By identifying, financing and nurturing entrepreneurs in the digital health space, we repeat our successes and create significant value for our investors."

[Sector] **Healthtech**

[Description]
Founded in 2014 by Dr. Christoph Kausch and two other partners, MTIP has since invested all over Europe. Although it is headquartered in Basel, it is not exclusive to Switzerland and its portfolio includes companies from all over the continent. MTIP invests in companies that modernize the healthcare industry through digitalization. These include digital health, healthcare IT and medical technology companies with a digital focus. Through its investments, MTIP empowers these companies to grow and become global healthtech leaders. A prerequisite for companies is that they can provide clear health-related economic benefits.

MTIP is a growth capital investor, meaning that companies must already have market traction and usually around €5 million plus of revenues when the investment is made. MTIP helps companies in the development stage to further scale up and grow by investing up to €25 million per company. An example would be an initial €10 million plus investment, that would then be followed up by further investments, depending on the specific company and its targets. "We know how to scale up companies, as well as the typical pitfalls they can avoid," says managing partner Dr. Christoph Kausch.

In addition to financial investment, MTIP also offers expert advice to help companies grow and succeed. MTIP partners with the management team of the companies it invests in and is delighted to use the expertise of its staff members to help startups throughout the transformative process.

[Apply to] **mtip.ch/contact**

[Links] Web: **mtip.ch** LinkedIn: **company/mtip-healthtech-investors** Twitter: **@MTIP_CH**

- **Have a dynamite pitch deck.**
  We get a lot of applications, so we make initial decisions based on pitch decks. To stand out from the crowd, yours must be easy to understand without an accompanying presentation.

- **Have a sound business plan and do your homework.**
  We want to see a Gantt chart with financial planning and timing of programs, as well as a high-level competitive analysis in your initial pitch deck.

- **Be passionate.**
  We look for inspiring founders as well as ideas. Tell us what excites you about your data.

- **Be a good communicator and know your audience.**
  You need to be able to transmit your idea clearly to any nonexpert scientist right from the word go.

Novartis Venture Fund

[Name]

[Elevator Pitch] *"We make equity investments in biotech and biopharma companies that develop novel, high-impact therapeutics to address significant unmet medical needs in a range of diseases. The aim is to foster innovation, drive patient benefit and generate returns."*

[Sector] **Healthcare**

[Description] Novartis Venture Fund invests in biotech and biopharma companies at any stage in the US, Europe and Israel. Based in Basel, it has an in-depth understanding of the local community, as well as high-level expertise in drug discovery and development. It seeks highly innovative ideas with transformative potential that can become the new therapeutic standard of care or answer significant unmet medical needs in a range of therapeutic areas. Its current portfolio is strong in oncology and actively diversifying into areas including immunology, ophthalmology, neuroscience, cardiovascular medicine, metabolics and more. Funding proposals are usually submitted directly by startup founders, arrive through the fund's investor and academic network or are a result of connections made at conferences.

With a fund of around $750 million, Novartis Venture Fund's strategy is to make larger equity investments in drug discovery and development. While these can occur at any stage, the sweet spot is hands-on company formation and early preclinical-stage drug discovery, with a strong commitment to follow-on investments. Funding amounts are case-by-case, but typical investments are $1 million–$5 million for seed funding and $7 million–$12 million for Series A or B. Total investments over the course of a company's activity may reach $30 million.

When considering new proposals and assessing a company's business plan, scientific rationale and data, the fund places a lot of importance on founders and teams, especially with early-stage companies. In addition to scientific excellence and originality, it looks for determination, openness and willingness to listen to advice. The latter is crucial, as Novartis Venture Fund typically leads or coleads investments and plays an active role on company boards. Coinvestment partners frequently include other corporate venture funds. With one of the most diverse teams in the sector, it also values diversity in the founders and teams it works with.

[Apply to] info.nvf@nvfund.com

[Links] Web: **nvfund.com** Twitter: **@NVF_VC**

directory

The following selection is a brief choice of organizations, companies and contacts available in the Basel Area

Startups

Alentis Therapeutics
Hochbergerstr. 60C
4057 Basel
alentis.ch

ARTIDIS
Hochbergerstr. 60C
4057 Basel
artidis.com

InnoSpina
Place des Sciences 2
2822 Courroux
innospina.com

MyCamper
Steinenvorstadt 79
4051 Basel
mycamper.ch

Mycrobez
Grellingerstr. 27
4052 Basel
mycrobez.ch

NextDay.Vision
Place des Sciences 2
2822 Courroux
nextday.vision

Nutrix
Lichtstr. 35
4056 Basel
nutrix.tech

Synendos Therapeutics
Gewerbestr. 24
4123 Allschwil
synendos.com

TOLREMO
Hofackerstr. 40b
4132 Muttenz
tolremo.com

Typewise
Im Kugelfang 50
4102 Binningen
typewise.app

Programs

100 fürs Baselbiet
Rheinstr. 7
4410 Liestal
100fuersbb.ch

BaseLaunch
Dufourstr. 11
4010 Basel
baselaunch.ch

Business Park
Oberbaselbiet | Laufental
| Thierstein
Riedstr. 6
4222 Zwingen
bplt.ch/kostenlose-beratung

DayOne
Dufourstr. 11
4010 Basel
dayone.swiss

i4Challenge
Dufourstr. 11
4010 Basel
i4challenge.com

Innolab by Roche
F. Hoffmann-La Roche AG
Konzern Hauptsitz
Grenzacherstr. 124
4070 Basel
roche.com

Standortförderung Baselland
StartUp@Baselland
Amtshausgasse 7
4410 Liestal
startup-baselland.ch

Startup Academy
Picassoplatz 4
4052 Basel
startup-academy.ch

Swiss Innovation Challenge
Haus der Wirtschaft
Hardstr. 1
4133 Pratteln
swissinnovationchallenge.ch

Swiss Startup Challenge
FHNW University of Applied
Sciences and Arts
Northwestern Switzerland
School of Business
Institute of Management
Bahnhofstr. 6
5210 Windisch
fhnw.ch/startupchallenge

Swiss Sustainability Challenge
Fachhochschule
Nordwestschweiz FHNW
Bahnhofstr. 6
5210 Windisch
sustainabilitychallenge.ch

Spaces

The 5th Floor
Hofackerstr. 40B
4132 Muttenz
the5thfloor.ch

Business Parc Reinach
Christoph Merian-Ring 11
4153 Reinach
businessparc.ch

Impact Hub Basel
Münchensteinerstr. 274a
4053 Basel
basel.impacthub.net

The Manhattan
Route de Moutier 9
2800 Delémont
themanhattan.ch

Switzerland Innovation Park Basel Area
Gewerbestr. 24, 2nd Floor
4123 Allschwil
switzerland-innovation.com/baselarea

Technologiepark Basel
Hochbergerstr. 60C
4057 Basel
technologiepark.ch

Some of the websites in the Directory require the 'www' prefix.

Westhive
Rosentalstr. 33
4058 Basel
westhive.com

Experts

Baloise Group
Aeschengraben 21
4002 Basel
baloise.com

Basler Kantonalbank
Postfach
4002 Basel
bkb.ch

Novartis Pharma
Postfach
Basel
novartis.com

Wild Ma-Gässli
wildma.ch

Founders

Bioversys
c/o Technologiepark
Hochbergerstr. 60c
4057 Basel
bioversys.com

Clarena
Peter Merian-Str. 45
4052 Basel
clarena.net

Idorsia
Hegenheimermattweg 91
4123 Allschwil
idorsia.com

Resistell
Hofackerstr. 40B
4132 Muttenz
resistell.com

Schools

**FHNW University
of Applied Sciences and Arts
Northwestern Switzerland**
Bahnhofstr. 6
5210 Windisch
fhnw.ch

Haute École Arc
Espace de l'Europe 11
CH-2000 Neuchâtel
he-arc.ch

University of Basel
Petersplatz 1
Postfach
4001 Basel
unibas.ch

Unternehmer Campus
Elisabethenstr. 23
4. OG
4051 Basel
campus-unternehmertum.ch

Investors

HEMEX
Kasernenstr. 30
4410 Liestal
hemex.ch

MTIP
Dufourstr. 49
4052 Basel
mtip.ch

Novartis Venture Fund
c/o Novartis International
Postfach
4002 Basel
nvfund.com

Startup Support

NewCo Switzerland SA
Rue des Côtes-de-
-Montbenon 5
1003 Lausanne
newco.ch

StadtKonzeptBasel
Grenzacherstr. 79
4058 Basel
Stadtkonzeptbasel.ch

Media Partner

Swisspreneur
Elias-Canetti-Str. 87
8050 Zürich
swisspreneur.org

Accommodation

immobilier.ch
immobilier.ch

ImmoScout24
immoscout24.ch

homegate
homegate.ch

newhome
newhome.ch

Banks

Basler Kantonalbank
bkb.ch

**Basellandschaftliche
Kantonalbank**
blkb.ch

CIC
cic.ch

Coffee Shops and Places with Wifi

Brewery of Franches-Montagnes SA
Chemin des Buissons 8
2350 Saignelégier
brasseriebfm.ch/en

Café Frühling
Klybeckstr. 69
4057 Basel
cafe-fruehling.ch

Stageclub
Rue Emile-Boéchat 71
2800 Delémont
stageclubdelemont.com/
la-plage

Financial Services

Finium
Henric Petri-Str. 11
4051 Basel

Herzog-Treuhand
Brotkorbstr. 1
4332 Stein
herzog-treuhand.ch

TRETOR
Industriestr. 7
4410 Liestal
tretor.ch

Groups and Meetups

American Women's Club of Basel
awcbasel.org

Centrepoint Basel
centrepoint.ch

Internations Basel
internations.org/basel-expats

Professional Women's Group of Basel
pwg-basel.ch

Important Government Offices

Bevölkerungsdienste und Migration Basel-Stadt
Spiegelgasse 6
4001 Basel
bdm.bs.ch

Economic Development Basel-Stadt: Amt für Wirtschaft und Arbeit
Utengasse 36
4005 Basel
awa.bs.ch/
standortfoerderung.html

Economic Development Baselland
Amtshausgasse 7
4410 Liestal
economy-bl.ch

Insurance Companies

Die Mobiliar - General Agency Liestal
Burgstr. 6
4410 Liestal
mobiliar.ch

Language Schools

Academia Basel
Schifflände 3
4051 Basel
academia-basel.ch

Allgemeine Gewerbeschule Basel
Vogelsangstr. 15, Postfach
4005 Basel
agsbs.ch/ausbildung/
weiterbildung

ARCADIA Bildungscampus
Weisse Gasse 6
4001 Basel
arcadia-bildungscampus.ch

GGG Kurse
Eisengasse 5
4051 Basel
ggg-kurse.ch

Inlingua Basel
Dufourstr. 50
4052 Basel
inlingua-basel.ch

Lycée cantonal de Porrentruy
Place Blarer-de-Wartensee 2
2900 Porrentruy
lycee.ch

Miteinander Vorwärts
Jutta Kressibucher
Kornfeldstr. 52
4125 Riehen
deutsch-sprechen.ch

Strate J - Campus de formation tertiaire
Route de Moutier 14
2800 Delémont
stratej.ch

Integration Classes

GGG Migration
ggg-migration.ch

InterNations
internations.org

Startup Events

Basel Area Business & Innovation
baselarea.swiss/basel-events

Entrepreneurs Club of the University of Basel
eventbrite.com/o/
university-of
-basel-14794586208

Impact Hub Basel Events
impacthubbasel.eventbrite
.com

Jungunternehmerpreis Nordwestschweiz
jungunternehmerpreis.ch

Swiss Innovation Challenge
swissinnovationchallenge.ch

Swiss Innovation Forum
swiss-innovation.com

Event Spaces

Altes Kraftwerk
alteskraftwerk.ch

BAU3
bau3.ch

Holzpark Klybeck
holzpark-klybeck.ch

Launchlabs Basel
launchlabs.ch/de

Philosophicum
philosophicum.ch

Hotel Les Troi Rois, Basel-Stadt

glossary

A

accelerator — an organization or program that offers advice and resources to help small businesses grow

AI (artificial intelligence) — the simulation of human intelligence by computer systems; machines that are able to perform tasks normally carried out by humans

angel investment — outside funding with shared ownership equity typically made possible by an affluent individual who provides a startup with starting capital

[see also: **business angel**]

B

bootstrapping — to self-fund, without outside investment

business angel — an experienced entrepreneur or professional who provides starting or growth capital for promising startups

[see also: **angel investment**]

C

CEO (chief executive officer) — the highest-ranking person in a company, responsible for taking on managerial decisions

clinical development candidate — a pre-clinical licensed product that possesses desirable properties of a therapeutic agent for the treatment of a clinical condition

COO (chief operating officer) — a high-level executive running the operations of a company

coworking space — a shared working environment

E

early-stage — the stage in which financing is provided by a venture capital firm to a company after the seed round; a company stage in which a product or service is still in development but not on the market yet

elevator pitch — a short description of an idea, product or company that explains the concept

exit — a way to transition the ownership of a company to another company

F

fintech — financial technology; a technology or innovation that aims to compete with traditional financial methods in the delivery of financial services

flex desk — a shared desk available for temporary use in a coworking space

I

incubator — a facility established to nurture young startup firms during their first few months or years of development

Industry 4.0 — the ongoing automation of traditional manufacturing and industrial practices using modern smart technology

IoT (Internet of Things) — the network of physical objects that are embedded with sensors, software and other technologies used for the purpose of connecting and exchanging data with other devices and systems over the internet

IP (intellectual property) — property which is not tangible; the result of creativity, such as ideas that can be patented and protected by copyright

L

later-stage — the stage in which companies have typically demonstrated viability as a going concern and have a product with a strong market presence

M

M&A (mergers and acquisitions) — a merger is a process by which two companies join to form a new company, while an acquisition is the purchase of one company by another where no new company is formed

MVP (minimum viable product) — a product with just enough features to satisfy early customers who can provide feedback for future product development

N

novel resistance modulator — the target that needs to be inhibited in order to prevent the development of resistance

O

OEM (original equipment manufacturer) — an organization that makes devices from component parts bought from other organizations

P

pitch — an opportunity to introduce a business idea in a limited amount of time to potential investors, often using a presentation

pivot — the process when a company quickly changes direction after previously targeting a different market segment

product-market fit — a product that has created significant customer value and its best target industries have been identified

S

scaleup — a company that has already validated its product in a market and is economically sustainable

SDGs (sustainable development goals) — a United Nations agenda that covers seventeen global goals that can be achieved by reaching 169 defined targets

SDG indicators — an indication used to measure the progress in reaching the Sustainable Development Goals

[see also: **UN Goals for Sustainable Development and sustainable development**]

seed funding — the first round of venture capital funding (typically called the seed round); a small, early-stage investment from family members, friends, banks or an investor, also known as a seed investor

series A/B/C/D — the subsequent funding rounds that come after the seed stage and aim to raise further capital (up to $1 million) when the company demonstrates various increase factors

startup — companies under three years old that are in the growth stage and starting to become profitable (if not already)

sustainable development — defined by the UN World Commission on Environment and Development as an organizing principle that "meets the needs of the present without compromising the ability of future generations to meet their own needs."

U

UN Goals for Sustainable Development (SDG) — Seventeen intergovernmental development goals established by all 193 members of the United Nations in 2015 for the year 2030. The SDGs' non-binding targets provide a framework for organizations and businesses to think about and begin addressing the world's most important challenges

[see also: **SDGs and sustainable development**]

USP (unique selling point) — a factor that differentiates a product from its competitors

UX (user experience design) — the process of designing and improving user satisfaction with products so that they are useful, easy to use and pleasurable to interact with

V

VC (venture capital) — a form of financing that comes from a pool of investors in a venture capital firm in return for equity

STARTUP GUIDE JOHANNESBURG — The Entrepreneur's Handbook
STARTUP GUIDE HAMBURG — The Entrepreneur's Handbook
STARTUP GUIDE AMSTERDAM — The Entrepreneur's Handbook
STARTUP GUIDE CAPE TOWN — The Entrepreneur's Handbook
STARTUP GUIDE LUXEMBOURG — The Entrepreneur's Handbook
STARTUP GUIDE VIENNA — The Entrepreneur's Handbook
STARTUP GUIDE TEL AVIV — The Entrepreneur's Handbook
STARTUP GUIDE MADRID — The Entrepreneur's Handbook
STARTUP GUIDE COPENHAGEN — The Entrepreneur's Handbook
IMPACT GUIDE SERIES · STARTUP GUIDE JAPAN — The Entrepreneur's Handbook
STARTUP GUIDE PARIS — The Entrepreneur's Handbook
STARTUP GUIDE LOS ANGELES — The Entrepreneur's Handbook
STARTUP GUIDE REYKJAVIK — The Entrepreneur's Handbook
STARTUP GUIDE STOCKHOLM — The Entrepreneur's Handbook
STARTUP GUIDE MUNICH — The Entrepreneur's Handbook
STARTUP GUIDE FRANKFURT — The Entrepreneur's Handbook
STARTUP GUIDE ZURICH — The Entrepreneur's Handbook
STARTUP GUIDE LONDON — The Entrepreneur's Handbook
STARTUP GUIDE TOKYO — The Entrepreneur's Handbook
STARTUP GUIDE LISBON — The Entrepreneur's Handbook
IMPACT GUIDE SERIES · STARTUP GUIDE SWITZERLAND — The Entrepreneur's Handbook
STARTUP GUIDE SINGAPORE — The Entrepreneur's Handbook
STARTUP GUIDE NEW YORK — The Entrepreneur's Handbook
IMPACT GUIDE SERIES · STARTUP GUIDE EGYPT — The Entrepreneur's Handbook
STARTUP GUIDE BANGKOK — The Entrepreneur's Handbook
STARTUP GUIDE BERLIN — The Entrepreneur's Handbook
IMPACT GUIDE SERIES · STARTUP GUIDE LAGOS — The Entrepreneur's Handbook
IMPACT GUIDE SERIES · STARTUP GUIDE ACCRA — The Entrepreneur's Handbook
IMPACT GUIDE SERIES · STARTUP GUIDE NAIROBI — The Entrepreneur's Handbook
IMPACT GUIDE SERIES · STARTUP GUIDE GERMANY — The Entrepreneur's Handbook
IMPACT GUIDE SERIES · STARTUP GUIDE KIGALI — The Entrepreneur's Handbook

startupguide.com   Follow us: @StartupGuideHQ

About the Guide

Based on traditional guidebooks and stocked with information you might need to know about starting your next business adventure, Startup Guide books help you navigate and connect with different startup scenes across the globe. Each book is packed with exciting stories of entrepreneurship, insightful interviews with local experts and useful tips and tricks. To date, Startup Guide has featured over fifty cities and regions in Europe, Asia, the US, Africa and the Middle East, including Berlin, London, Singapore, New York, Cape Town and Tel Aviv.

How we make the books:

To ensure an accurate and trustworthy guide every time, we team up with local partners that are established in their respective startup scene. We then ask the local community to nominate startups, coworking spaces, founders, schools, investors, incubators and established businesses to be featured through an online submission form. Based on the results, these submissions are narrowed down to the top one hundred organizations and individuals. Next, the local advisory board – which is selected by our community partners and consists of key players in the local startup community – votes for the final selection, ensuring a balanced representation of industries and startup stories in each book.
The local community partners then work in close collaboration with our international editorial and design team to help research, organize interviews with journalists and plan photoshoots. Finally, all content is reviewed and edited and the book is designed and created by the Startup Guide team before going to print in Berlin.

Where to find us:

The easiest way to get your hands on a Startup Guide book is to order it from our online shop: startupguide.com/shop. You can also visit us at our office:

Borgbjergsvej 1
2450 Copenhagen, Denmark
copenhagen@startupguide.com

Want to become a stockist or suggest a store?

Get in touch here: sales@gestalten.com

The Startup Guide Website

Since the first Startup Guide book was published, our network has grown and the possibilities to reach new audiences have expanded. One of the reasons we decided to start producing content through a digital platform was to be able to take a deeper look at the cities, regions and ecosystems that our books cover. We want to make it more accessible for new entrepreneurs to understand the process of getting a startup off the ground through the stories of those who were once in their shoes. By sharing educational content and inspiring examples from the startup community, our website provides valuable insights and continues our core purpose: to guide, empower and inspire people beginning their entrepreneurial path.

For more details, visit our website at startupguide.com.

#startupeverywhere

Startup Guide was founded by Sissel Hansen in 2014. As a publishing and media company, we produce guidebooks and online content to help entrepreneurs navigate and connect with different startup scenes across the globe. As the world of work changes, our mission stays the same: to guide, empower and inspire people to start their own business anywhere. To get your hands on one of our books, feel free to visit us at our office in Copenhagen.

Want to learn more,
become a partner or just say hello? ♥

Send us an email at info@startupguide.com

Follow us: @StartupGuideHQ

Join us and #startupeverywhere

With thanks to our **Content Partners**

Wild Ma-Gässli

Our **Startup Support**

NewCo

And our **Media Partner**

"With customer service and continual improvement at the heart of NewCo, the organization has so far helped more than a thousand startups and entrepreneurs."

Startup Support
/ NewCo Switzerland SA

[Elevator Pitch] *"We help entrepreneurs and startups with the formation of their own company. Using a software-enabled service we make it easy, fast and safe for our customers to start their own business."*

Founded in 2020, NewCo Switzerland SA (NewCo) simplifies the administration process of setting up a new business and helps entrepreneurs to form, modify or transform a company. It was established after the founders encountered difficulties in setting up their own new enterprise in Switzerland. They found the setup process was complicated and expensive, took months to complete and that there was little advice or transparency about how to actually start a business. Following this experience and having researched the market, they realized that there was an opportunity to create a service that would help entrepreneurs and startups in a quick and easy manner. They wanted to create an offer that was safe and easy to use, had no hidden costs and that could be completed in a few minutes.

With customer service and continual improvement at the heart of NewCo, the organization has so far helped more than a thousand startups and entrepreneurs. From the formation of businesses to changes in the commercial register, its services are continually expanding. It also offers company transformations and a web application that allows online signature legalization. The team is always looking for ways to improve the company's products and seeking out ways to adapt and use technology to provide an agile and innovative service to its customers.

NewCo also works with several partner organizations that promote entrepreneurship or assist new business, and each partner offers an exclusive discount to NewCo customers. Its long-term goal is to become the one-stop shop for all legal matters for entrepreneurs looking to start and grow their companies in Switzerland.

[Links]   Web: newco.ch LinkedIn: company/newcoswitzerland Twitter: @newco_ch
Facebook: newcoswitzerland Instagram: newcoswitzerland

Startup Support
/ StadtKonzeptBasel

[Elevator Pitch] *"As a city-management organization, our goal is to support our local community to make Basel an attractive and sustainable destination. We love to work collaboratively with our members and partners to develop the city and its range of experiences."*

Founded in 1978, StadtKonzeptBasel – formerly Pro Innerstadt Basel – is a city-management organization committed to building and developing a diverse, vibrant and sustainable city. Through its solutions-oriented approach, it supports local retailers, restaurateurs, hoteliers, cultural and leisure businesses, homeowners and service providers in Basel Area. From offering founders advice on launching their business to helping companies develop unique offers and marketing strategies, StadtKonzeptBasel offers an array of services and acts as a supportive partner and sounding board for local individuals and companies. It also provides valuable connections and contacts to help organizations find suitable premises. StadtKonzeptBasel works collaboratively with its members and local businesses to make Basel an attractive destination for visitors, residents and businesses, and it strives to do so in a sustainable manner. Through its platforms, it shares its members' passion for the city and provides a daily dose of inspiration, as well as support for local communities.

StadtKonzeptBasel is responsible for organizing a range of events throughout the year, for both members and the local area. These events range from city-experience festivals to workshops and panel events, as well as themed events and campaigns such as LoveYourCity, which shares a passion and love for the area through inspirational content. The organization also oversees and manages the lifestyle platform BaselLive.ch, which is promoted through the local public transport system and highlights local businesses, events and experiences, and reaches around 500,000 commuters daily. StadtKonzeptBasel also produces BaselLive magazine, which is distributed to around 240,000 people in the Basel-Stadt and Baselland communities. It also operates StadtBonBasel gift vouchers, which can be purchased online and spent in local retail, gastronomy, and cultural outlets in the area; around CHF 9 million are turned over annually through the scheme.

[Links] Web: stadtkonzeptbasel.ch LinkedIn: company/stadtkonzeptbasel
Twitter: @StadtKonzeptBS Facebook: basellive.ch Instagram: basellive.ch

" *Swisspreneur targets predominantly young and ambitious entrepreneurs who dream of making an impact and are looking for the inspiration and practical, hands-on advice necessary to build a successful company.* "

Media Partner
/ Swisspreneur

Swisspreneur is a nonprofit on a mission to advance Swiss entrepreneurship. The main way that we do this is by producing top-quality podcast episodes that feature well-known Swiss founders and investors. On the podcast, we discuss a wide range of startup topics, from sales and marketing to fundraising, growth, operations and culture.

Swisspreneur was originally created in 2016 by Wildfire founder and ex-Googler Alain Chuard, and has since witnessed immense growth, with over 150 episodes released and an annual social media reach of over five million people. It has also become the number one business podcast in Switzerland.

With the intent of cultivating strong bonds within the Swiss ecosystem, Swisspreneur also frequently participates in startup events (such as Start Summit and Startup Days) and hosts regular Founders Dinners, where a community of founders comes together, whether remotely or face-to-face, for an evening of productive exchanges.

With its podcast episodes, newsletters and social media presence, Swisspreneur targets predominantly young and ambitious entrepreneurs who dream of making an impact and are looking for the inspiration and practical, hands-on advice necessary to build a successful company.

We have also launched the Swisspreneur Coaching Package, in which we draw from our network of experienced former podcast guests to provide Swiss founders with the area-specific expertise needed to grow their startup to the next level. From sales to fundraising, to culture and exit readiness, founders can book the coach that best fits their needs.

[Links]   Web: swisspreneur.org LinkedIn: company/swisspreneur Twitter: @swisspreneur
Facebook: swisspreneur Instagram: swisspreneur

WHERE NEXT?